THE
PRIVACY PLAN

THE
PRIVACY PLAN

How to Keep What You Own
Secret From High-Tech Snoops,
Lawyers and Con Men

ROBERT J. MINTZ
PETER S. DOFT

Published by Francis O'Brien & Sons Publishing Company, Inc.
1201 Camino Del Mar, Suite 203, Del Mar, California 92014
(800) 223-4291
rjmintz@rjmintz.com
www.privacyplan.com

This book is sold with the understanding that neither the publisher nor the authors are engaged in offering legal or other professional advice. Any actions with regard to the information contained in this book should be undertaken only with the advice and counsel of a trained legal professional.

Library of Congress Cataloging in Process.

ISBN 0-9639971-1-4

Printed in the United States of America.

Interior Design by The Roberts Group
Cover Design by Lee Noel

Contents

Introduction

Recent ADVANCES IN COMPUTER and Internet technology allow unprecedented access to your most sensitive personal and financial information. Detailed information describing all of your real estate and business interests, the name of your bank and brokerage firm, your account balances, and your transaction history can be accessed and assembled without your knowledge or permission. Now, anyone can find out what you have and how much you are worth.

These capabilities are a new phenomenon. Until recently, separate bits and pieces of information about your life were scattered in dusty file drawers and county records around the country. Your birth certificate, driving records, insurance file, marriage licenses, and loan applications were maintained or stored in written files, record books, or sometimes the computer at the office where the records were kept. *Information could not be accessed from outside the office where the records were stored.*

If you or somebody else wanted information from your birth certificate, you had to physically go to the records office in the county where you were born and look through the indexed records. An investigator attempting to assemble information about your life had to travel from one county courthouse to another, stand in line, search through library archives and public records, and hope to come up with some useful information. The process of gathering personal information was a laborious and expensive job.

But all of that has changed. The scraps of paper and the written records have been converted into an electronic form which can be stored and searched by a computer. And these computers and the databases have been connected through the Internet so that the information in any one computer can be accessed and searched from any other computer. If somebody wants to find out information about you, a single query will hunt through billions of documents stored on thousands of interconnected databases to produce a frighteningly thorough profile of your life. An investigator can now sit in the comfort of his office with a computer, a modem, and a cup of coffee in one hand, and in minutes he will have everything about you that he needs to know.

The accessibility of specific information about asset ownership creates direct and indirect threats, which can jeopardize financial security and physical safety. Detailed financial information including real estate and stock holdings and complete bank records can act as a magnet for lawsuits, frivolous claims, and unreasonable demands from a variety of sources.

In fact, this availability of financial information is the principle source of fuel for the "litigation explosion." Lawsuits and claims are often filed simply because it is known that the defendant is a "deep pocket" with the capacity to pay a judgment. Regardless of who is really responsible for the alleged wrong, the defendant will always be the party with the ability to pay a judgment. If someone is able to locate specific information about your assets, you become an attractive and vulnerable target for a lawsuit or claim. The most common and dangerous abuse of your financial information is related to the litigation process. Whether or not a lawsuit is filed as well as the strategy of the case depend largely on the ability to accurately determine what you have, where it is located, and how much it is worth.

Lawyers aren't the only ones who want to know what you have. Business associates and competitors may have a vital interest in learning how much you are making and where you are spending money. An ex-spouse may need information to bolster the case for an increase in alimony or support payments. An unhappy current spouse will be advised to find account balances and locations *before* serving the divorce papers. Criminals uncover and evaluate financial accounts in a variety of schemes to defraud unsuspecting victims. Perhaps an elderly parent or relative will be victimized by these practices.

Our solution to these problems is to develop legal strategies which accomplish two important objectives: The first goal is to create financial privacy. Nobody should be able to find out what you own unless you tell them. Information about your bank accounts, stocks, real estate, and business interests should not be accessible by any outside party. A properly designed financial privacy plan allows you to control the flow of your personal information—to keep it out of the hands of dangerous people.

Second, we want to construct a legal firewall around all of your valuable assets. We want to shield and insulate assets from the potential danger of lawsuits and claims. If you are the target of a lawsuit, for whatever reason, your property should be protected from a judgment.

During the past year, there has been a rash of media stories and Congressional hearings into the dangers caused by the availability of sensitive financial information. In response to this heightened awareness of the problem, we have witnessed an explosion of demand for legal strategies designed to protect financial privacy and shield personal assets from lawsuits and other attacks. A considerable portion of our practice over the last twenty years has been devoted to these issues, and this book is intended to present the solutions we have seen and developed over the years.

In chapters 1 and 2, we will show you how personal information about you is located. You will learn the tools and the techniques used by investigators and "information brokers" to uncover your bank accounts and other private financial data. We will look at the reasons why somebody wants this information about you—and what they can do with it to harm you.

In chapters 3 and 4, we will examine the lawsuit danger in greater detail. We will see how a lawyer uses private information about your financial matters to evaluate a case, and then what really happens during a lawsuit.

Beginning in chapter 5, we will turn our attention to the strategies that are commonly employed to achieve financial privacy and asset protection purposes. We will look at corporations, Limited Liability Companies, Family Limited Partnerships, and a variety of trust arrangements and offshore plans.

We will concentrate attention on a powerful strategy known as the *Privacy Trust*, which allows us to create an excellent level of privacy and asset protection in the most flexible and convenient format.

As a word of caution, this book cannot possibly substitute for competent legal advice. Our treatment of the law is general and is not intended as a comprehensive discussion of all relevant issues. The law in each state will vary to some extent, and the applicability of the law will depend upon your individual circumstances.

If you have a particular question about the information in this book:

1. Telephone us at (800) 223-4291.

2. Visit our Web site at www.rjmintz.com.

3. E-mail us at rjmintz@rjmintz.com.

We will try our best to assist you.

CHAPTER ONE

How Anyone Can Find Out What You Own

ALL OF YOUR SECRETS are for sale on the Internet. At least all of your important secrets—such as where you keep your money, how much you have, and what you own. That is the type of information that most people like to keep to themselves. It's called financial privacy, and it's supposed to be nobody else's business—strictly between you and Uncle Sam. But now, anyone can get a complete list of all of your bank and brokerage accounts, how much is in them, and where they are located. Property which you own anywhere in the country can be found with a simple computer keystroke.

Lawyers use these search techniques to find out if you have enough money to make it worthwhile to sue you. Lawyers hate to sue someone, win a judgment, and then discover there's not enough money to pay the award. They like to *first* make sure that you have resources before they spend their time chasing you around. This is especially important when the lawyer is working for a contingency fee.

The dangers posed by these privacy intrusions are facilitated by the ready access to information available on the Internet. The phenomenal increase in the amount of information and the speed with which it is distributed has produced dramatic changes in our business and personal lives. Facts and opinions are gathered, analyzed, and distributed in nanoseconds instead of days, weeks, and months. Although these new capabilities for assembling and distributing information can have an enormous and favorable impact on society, the result may not be so favorable *when the information that is being gathered and distributed is about you.* The intimate details from the private lives of public figures make great reading as they flash onto your computer screen and millions of others at the speed of light. It is quite another matter, however, when the information packet zipping through cyberspace is special delivering *your* Social Security number and *your* mother's maiden name into the hands of *your* ex-wife's lawyer.

In this chapter, we will examine the type of personal information about you which is available. We will describe who is involved in the business and how they discover sensitive financial information that you probably do not want others to know. Later we will show you how to protect yourself from these tactics, but first let's see what we are up against.

Searching For Your Real Estate

Anyone wishing to put together a complete picture of your assets will first locate and value any property which you own. Until recently, a comprehensive and accurate search such as this was difficult or impossible. Even six or seven years ago there were no state-wide or national database listings of real estate owners. Deeds to property were filed in the recorder's office in the county where the property was located. The deed was manually indexed by the clerks. If someone wanted to find out what property you owned, they would have to go to the local recorder's office and look in the Grantee Index under your name. (Grantee is a legal term for the purchaser in a real estate transaction.) That index would show any property, located in that county, which had been deeded to you. Property in a different county would not be found in that index.

An investigator attempting to find all real estate which you owned had the daunting task of searching the index for every county. To make sure that all of your real estate was discovered, an investigator had to search every county in the country. He, or someone working for him, had to personally go to the recorder's office to look up the information. If he had good sources, he might be able to call on the phone and get a clerk to check the records. In either case, it was a time-consuming, expensive, and inefficient process.

About fifteen years ago, we had a client who was trying to collect a $1 million judgment from a former business partner we'll call Jake. Wisely, Jake was staying out of sight to avoid our subpoena. We wanted to bring him into court for a debtor's examination to make him tell us what he owned. We knew he had substantial assets, but we couldn't find him or any of his property. A search of all of the county real estate records in Los Angeles—where he lived—and each surrounding county showed nothing. Since there was a lot of money involved, we paid thousands of dollars to search every county in California, Nevada, Washington, and Oregon. Still nothing.

One day, after five or six years of basically futile efforts, we received a call from a former secretary who used to work in our office. She had left the firm to open an art gallery in Vail, Colorado. "Are you still looking for that Jake guy?" she asked. "I just saw him on the ski slopes." That was a great tip. We checked the county records and found a house in his name that he had purchased for $3.6 million in cash. We immediately entered our judgment in Colorado and filed a lien on the property. Jake settled quickly and our client ended up with about $2.7 million, covering the judgment, interest, and court costs. Jake had figured we would never find the property, and without our lucky break, he would have been right.

It doesn't take luck anymore to find somebody's real estate. Almost every county has computerized its records, and the information has been linked to a national database. Instead of visiting every county recorder or trying to guess where property is located, with a single query, a computer search retrieves all of the real estate records in your name—compiled from every state and county in the country. The report identifies the cost of the property, the loan balance, and the type of property. This information is produced in minutes, and the cost is nominal.

Discovering Your Financial Accounts

After locating your real estate, the investigator will search for your cash. Discovering the existence and details concerning bank accounts and brokerage accounts appears more complex than tracing real estate records. Unlike real estate, a financial account is *supposed* to be a private matter. A banker is someone you should be able to trust with your money. By tradition, the relationship between a bank and a customer implies a level of discretion and confidentiality that can be breached only under extreme circumstances. Although no one expects that their account is secret, in the Swiss style, the common understanding is that in the absence of some type of inquiry from the government or compulsion from a court, the bank will not make your account information available to third parties.

Unfortunately, anyone with expectations of any degree of privacy with respect to a financial account will be dangerously disappointed. Bank and brokerage accounts records are now easily accessible to those who have learned the basic "tricks of the trade." For a modest fee, companies specializing in these services can be hired to perform comprehensive asset searches. A detailed report will list the location, account number, current balance, deposits, and withdrawals for every account that you own. A listing of every check you have written on the account—with the payee and amount—is included in the report. For stock brokerage accounts, a complete transaction history can be obtained with every purchase, sale, and current holding. Monthly credit card transactions and safe deposit boxes can be located if desired.

Information Brokers

The number of companies specializing in providing this information has proliferated as Internet technology makes these searches faster and more efficient. In the business these firms are known as "information brokers." They prepare a detailed financial report about an individual subject at the request of a particular client. Or they may collect a broad list of names which meet specific financial characteristics. For example, a list can be developed with the name of every bank customer, over sixty-five years old, with more than $50,000 in a certificate of deposit. The information is sold by the company to a marketing firm targeting these individuals for a competing financial product.

There are now hundreds of these information brokers advertising their services on the Internet. An example of the services offered and the fees is provided on figure 1–1.

ASSET SEARCHES

FIGURE 1-1

Bank Account Locate—$120 ($30 no hit fee). This search provides you with the bank at which your subject has an account. Information that you must provide for this search is name, address, Social Security number, or tax ID number. Search results will (in most cases) be returned to you in 2–4 business days.

Nationwide Bank Account Search—$500. This search provides bank names and addresses, account types, and balances as of the day of the search. Information that you must provide for this search is name, Social Security number, or federal ID number. Search results will (in most cases) be returned to you in 4–6 business days.

Real Property Search—$60. This search provides real estate owned by an individual or business. This is a nationwide search. Information that you must provide for this search is name of individual or business. Search results will (in most cases) be returned to you in 24–48 hours.

Safe Deposit Boxes—$300 ($30 no hit fee). This search provides deposit box number and branch address for all boxes located. Information that you must supply for this search is name, address, Social Security number, or tax ID number. Search results will (in most cases) be returned to you in 4–6 business days.

Stocks, Mutual Funds, Major Brokerages—$360. This searches all brokerage and mutual fund houses and provides account number, address of institution, and value of account. Information that you must provide for this search is name, address, Social Security number, or tax ID number. Search results will (in most cases) be returned to you in 4–6 business days.

Complete Asset Search—$900. All assets are searched. Information that you must provide for this search is name, address, Social Security number, or tax ID number. Search results will be returned to you in 4–6 business days.

Credit Card Transactions—$250 per month. To search for monthly credit card transactions, you must provide name and account. Search results will (in most cases) be returned to you in 2–6 business days.

You can see from this information that the services are comprehensive and the fees are modest. For less than $1,000, a fairly complete search will be performed—including real estate holdings, bank and brokerage accounts, and safe deposit boxes. A number of the firms advertising on the Web declare, "No find. No fee." If they fail to locate accounts in the search, for whatever reason, they do not charge for the service.

At these prices it is also clear that there is not a significant amount of time or labor involved in developing the reports. It is not necessary to bribe bank officials or employees or to send operatives on covert missions to steal protected bank files. An experienced investigator can gather the requested information with a computer and a telephone within a few minutes or hours.

In connection with our own legal practice, we decided to invest some money and create several tests to see what the investigators could find. We were refining our own strategies for protecting financial privacy and wanted to see exactly what we were up against. We wanted to know the most advanced techniques the investigators used and how deeply into a given structure they could penetrate.

We selected a close friend of ours, Steve, to be the subject of the investigation. He agreed, but we are not using his real name. Steve is a good subject because he has financial accounts, properties, and business interests which range from straightforward to fairly complex. We were interested in seeing which assets could be found. Here is the description of what he owns.

1. Five single family rental houses in California, Texas, and Arizona.

2. Joint checking account with his wife at a California bank.

3. Business checking account—with his signature only—in California.

4. Brokerage accounts with stocks and mutual funds at two different firms.

5. Account in the name of a Nevada corporation at a bank in Las Vegas. Steve is the owner of the company and one of three signatories on the account.

To perform this search, we chose a firm at random from several hundred advertising "Financial Investigations" on the Web. We told the investigator, a woman named Julia, that one of our clients was considering filing a lawsuit against Steve and we wanted to know beforehand exactly what he owned. Julia said she did these type of searches for many lawyers and helpfully suggested that we do a national search of real estate, bank accounts, stocks, and mutual funds for a fee of $600. We supplied the name of the subject— (Steve) and his Social Security number. If we had not known the Social Security number, the firm would have provided it for an extra $35. We also asked for the location of any safe deposit boxes.

Three days later we received a faxed report from Julia which contained the following information:

1. Steve's full legal name and the names of his wife and two children.

2. His current and previous addresses and place of employment.

3. Each of the five real estate properties was listed with street address, legal description, purchase price, loan balance, and estimated value.

4. The joint account and business checking account were identified by account number, bank branch, and current

balance. An additional account was located which Steve had forgotten he had; it contained $45.67. We were particularly impressed because this account was in Maine—Steve had opened it when vacationing there ten years earlier—and there had been no activity since that time.

5. Both of the brokerage accounts were listed. The report contained all of the stocks and mutual funds with the account balance and deposits for the month. Julia noted that a list of all purchases and sales for the year could be obtained for an additional $95.

6. Similarly, the Nevada corporation did nothing to shield the ownership of the bank account. Complete details, with the name of each signatory, was provided. We were supplied, without charge, the names and addresses of the corporate officers and directors.

7. As you might expect from the results so far, Steve's safe deposit box was located, with box number, bank, and branch. To the best of our knowledge, the contents of the box were not revealed.

These results were interesting to us. Even though the accounts were held in different forms and at different financial institutions, each had been discovered. In subsequent tests using ourselves and willing friends as guinea pigs, a total of fourteen out of sixteen possible accounts were accurately located.

For a story in *Parade Magazine,* author Peter Maas researched the availability of personal financial information and had an experience similar to ours. He retained an investigation firm to see what facts about himself could be uncovered. He gave the company forty-eight hours to produce telephone records for an unlisted phone number and bank records for each account he owned, in his name or with his wife. Within the indicated time, the company produced all three unlisted telephone numbers, together with a complete list of all of the toll calls made from each line. The financial accounts were also quickly discovered. "All my bank-account information—the account numbers, the banks involved, balances, and deposits for the previous month—was disturbingly accurate," Maas reported.

A recent front page article in the *Wall Street Journal* detailed the ease with which private investigators discovered accurate bank balances for customer accounts at financial institutions throughout the country—including the bank giants Fleet Financial, BankAmerica Corp., Bank of New York Co., Chase Manhattan Corp., Citibank, Great Western (now Washington Mutual), and PNC Bank Corp.

The article highlighted the stories of several individuals who were dismayed to learn that their accounts had been located and the balances disclosed—without their knowledge. The case of Dale Ohmart, a New Hampshire minister, was particularly striking. After his automobile struck a bicyclist, a local attorney, Frank Federico, acting on behalf of his client, retained an investigator to search for Ohmart's bank accounts. As quoted in the article, Federico said he hired the investigation firm because "we don't like to go after people individually unless they have liquid assets." Within a short time, the investigator provided Federico with account numbers and balances on four of Ohmart's accounts at Fleet Financial. Based upon the small balances in the account, Federico chose not to pursue the case. The article concludes, "Mr. Ohmart, age thirty-nine, didn't know that his account confidentiality had been violated until he was contacted for this article. He now says that he is considering closing his Fleet Financial accounts, and asks, 'How in the world can I feel that the relationship I have with the bank is secure or that my own assets are secure?'."

How They Find Your Accounts

There are three basic tools that investigators use to locate bank and brokerage accounts:

1. Sources.

2. Pretext.

3. Individual reference services, also known as "look-ups" or "locators."

As we know from our own experience, in most cases, one or the other of these tactics will produce the desired information.

Sources

The term "source" refers to an individual with access to the records of the financial institution. Generally this is a person who works for a particular firm and is willing to supply information about customer accounts. The source can be any employee with access to a computer terminal. All customer account records of the firm can usually be accessed from any terminal. By typing in the customer name, all account records can be located. The source usually receives a monthly salary or a per transaction fee. An investigator working on a case calls his source at Firm A—one of the largest brokerage firms—and says do you have any accounts for John Doe? If yes, he gets a list of the account numbers with whatever other information was requested by the client. If the answer is no, he goes down the list to Firm B and so on. Ninety-five percent of all brokerage accounts are held by the ten largest firms so most of the time the investigator will be successful quickly.

These networks of sources belong to a few well-heeled investigation companies. It requires a large investment and a steady flow of business to develop and maintain a sizable organization. A lot of energy and money is devoted to keeping these networks in place and operating smoothly. Most private investigation firms are small, one person operations, and they don't have the capital to create their own networks. Instead, they farm out the work to the big companies for a fee.

For example, you call Sam's Detective Agency and ask for a brokerage account search on your father-in-law, Arnie, which will cost $400. Sam doesn't have enough money or business to build his own source network, so he calls one of the handful of large companies who specialize in these searches. Sam pays $300 to X Company, and a clerk there simultaneously e-mails the request to X Company's contacts at more than 1,200 brokerage firms. Any firm that you can think of is covered by this list. Each source performs a quick computer check to see if Arnie is a customer and e-mails a positive or negative response. The turnaround time for all 1,200 firms can be less than an hour.

Sam gets the results that he asked for and delivers to you the finished report showing that Arnie has a stock brokerage account with more than $1 million. You don't know how Sam did it, and he won't tell you. He would not want you to bypass him and go directly to the information wholesaler. At the same time, Sam doesn't know who X Company's sources are—that's its secret. X Company would not want Sam to go directly to a source for information so it closely guards its valuable names. It is a sound business model that works efficiently for all of the parties involved. Everyone is satisfied—except, of course, Arnie.

Sources are also useful in acquiring telephone records from the phone companies which provide a wealth of detailed private information in a single complete package. Once the investigator has obtained a list of your toll calls, he uses a *reverse directory* to look up the names and addresses on the other end of each telephone call. Telephone records for a business or even some individuals can involve thousands of listed calls. Rather than calling each number to see who it belongs to, a reverse directory CD-ROM or Internet service can be used to list the identifying information in seconds.

Financial accounts are often located simply by a review of the list of names produced by the reverse directory. If you have called your bank on the telephone or conducted online banking from your computer modem, your telephone records provide an excellent trail leading directly to the bank's door. Account information is then determined by a source at the bank, or by pretext, using your identifying information.

Pretext

If Sam does not want to pay out a big chunk of his fee to X Company, he has to use a different strategy to find the information. The tactic is called *pretext*. Posing as Arnie, over the Internet or the telephone, he will attempt to gather the necessary account information.

Here's how the pretext scheme works: When you hired Sam to investigate Arnie's assets, Sam requested Arnie's full name and address. With this information, he then located Arnie's Social Security number. This is the key to all asset searches. It unlocks the door to almost every other piece of information, and it's easily accessible.

It is easier to find a Social Security number than an address or telephone number. Almost everyone has applied for credit and has provided their Social Security number on the application. The information on the applications are used to create databases, which are available for marketing and commercial purposes. For example, every individual credit report maintained by the three national credit agencies—Trans Union, Equifax, and Experion—contains a "credit header," which is the portion of the report with the name, aliases, birth date, current and prior addresses, telephone number, and Social Security number. Credit headers may be sold to services that compile information databases on millions of people. In a promotional brochure one service, People Finder, claims that its database contains credit header information on "160 million individuals, 92 million households, 71 million telephone numbers, and 40 million deceased records."

Sam maintains a subscription to several database suppliers, and he finds Arnie's Social Security number, mother's maiden name, and telephone numbers in a few minutes.

Sam then calls the customer service representatives at the firms, pretending that he is Arnie. The first task is simply to locate the accounts and the account number. One clever ruse is the *wire transfer ploy*. He may say, "This is Arnie Smith, and I would like to wire transfer $100,000 into my account. Can you please give me the proper routing instructions?"

The helpful employee, delighted that the bank will be receiving a large deposit, responds, "Certainly, Mr. Smith, let me just find your account here." If she can't find the account in the computer, she'll say, "I'm sorry, sir, but there must be some mistake. We can't find your account. Do you have the account number handy?" If she does find the account, she may ask for some verifying information such as date or place of birth or mother's maiden name. But Sam is prepared and he already has the right answer. She will then provide Sam with the routing information for the wire transfer, which will include the account number. Once Sam has the account number, that's the end of the ball game. He can now call and get whatever information he needs.

Although the telephone pretext strategy works well for broker-age firms, which are limited in number, these time-consuming techniques cannot be used when the requested search covers a large number of banks. It is not possible for the investigator to personally telephone even a fraction of the banks where the accounts might be located. And it is not cost effective to hire a room full of callers when the total fee is only a few hundred dollars.

Instead, Sam can use the high tech solution and can send a computer message to thousands of banks simultaneously—again posing as Arnie. Most banks now provide computerized responses to customer inquiries, and when the proper identifying data is furnished, the requested information can be elicited. Online Internet searches, in this manner, allow the investigator to cover banks throughout the country and to obtain account information quickly and inexpensively.

Pretext is often an effective technique for discovering account information even at supposedly safe offshore banks. An attorney friend of ours told us the story of a client who had stashed $2 million in an account at a Caribbean bank, in preparation for a nasty divorce. For a variety of reasons, there was no trail from the U.S. showing the transfer to the foreign bank so nothing in his banking records provided a tip-off for the wife. But her private investigator secured the husband's telephone records—ran a reverse directory check on the numbers—and found calls to a prominent overseas bank. Then, using a pretext strategy similar to the wire transfer ruse, he learned the account balance from the bank itself. Before this evidence could be presented to the judge—creating perjury and potential tax problems—the husband paid up—and far more than $2 million.

Many of the offshore banks—despite their purported secrecy—are as vulnerable to pretext calls as their American counterparts are. When the existence of the account is discovered through telephone records or other documents, experienced investigators will often be successful in obtaining the details that they are seeking.

Individual Reference Services

The booming demand for personal information has spawned a new multibillion dollar industry known as *individual reference services*—we'll call them *look-ups* for our discussion. Look-ups employ thousands of people, researching and inputting data, to supply personal information about individuals to attorneys, marketers, credit suppliers, financial institutions, and investigators. These companies compete to assemble ever larger and more comprehensive databases of personal information.

Rapid innovation creates awesomely powerful search techniques, combining and sorting information from multiple separate databases to produce a comprehensive personal information report. Instead of different searches for each important piece of data, a single search now presents a compilation of information from different sources. One look-up service claims that it takes any individual name and runs it through a thousand separate computer databases with more than *100 billion* stored records. According to the company, the average report length is 100 pages.

One hundred pages is a lot of information about you and probably covers just about everything you wouldn't want someone else to know. Besides the commonly available records of Social Security number, date of birth, and mother's maiden name, additional information also may include: place of birth, names and ages of family members and neighbors, schools attended, telephone numbers (listed and unlisted), employment information (past and present), physical characteristics, licenses held, voter registration information, driver's license number, automobile registration, personal identification numbers, association membership, census information associated with the addresses, and asset ownership. A newspaper archives search for any articles with your name may be included in the report.

The information compiled by the look-up services is derived from three principle sources:

1. Information which you have supplied.

2. Information from the public record.

3. Information from proprietary sources.

Voluntary Information

Much of the data about you which is available has been voluntarily furnished by you in connection with a service or a product that you purchased. What you probably didn't know was that the information would be made available for purposes other than those which you intended. For example, a mortgage loan application is a very sensitive document. It contains almost every detail of your private financial life, including tax returns and bank account statements. If the information from a mortgage application or other credit application is made available by employees at the lender or by the institution itself for marketing purposes, the material would be integrated into your personal file on the databases forever.

Unlike the credit reporting bureaus that are required by the Fair Credit Reporting Act to furnish you with a copy of your credit report under certain conditions and to correct errors on the report, the look-up services have no such obligations. The subject of a look-up search has no right to see or correct the information presented about him. You may be turned down for employment or insurance or some other service based on inaccurate information received from the look-up service without your knowledge. Unless you are able to subscribe to the particular service or obtain a report, you may never know the extent or the accuracy of the information presented about you.

Although not as comprehensive as the mortgage application, the totality of your subscriptions, warranty cards, purchases, survey responses, and other credit applications provides enough information about you to satisfy even the most diligent investigations. You have voluntarily provided your telephone numbers (listed and unlisted), your checking account number, credit cards, employment, and identifying information on a regular basis throughout your adult life. This information has been stored, assembled, merged, and regularly updated to provide a detailed picture of your personal and financial life.

Information from Public Records

The public records maintained by all levels of government are another rich source of information about you. Ownership of real estate, marriages and divorces, court records of civil and criminal cases, birth certificates, driving records and licenses, vehicle title and registration, voter registration, bankruptcy, incorporation, worker's compensation claims, firearm permits, professional and occupational licenses, and Uniform Commercial Code (UCC) and Security Exchange Commission (SEC) filings are a portion of the available information about you.

Each of these records provides an extraordinary level of insight into many areas of your life. For example, driver's license records contain accident reports, convictions, police reports, complaints, satisfied judgments, and hearing records in addition to the personal identifying information of age, sex, address, and physical appearance. Many states, such as New York, make these records available directly to the information services for a fee. Illinois sells its records for $10 million per year, and Rhode Island brings in $9.7 million just from the sale of its drivers' records. The records are provided directly in usable electronic form or are converted by vendors who then resell the information to the database services.

The information that is ultimately compiled by the look-up service is based upon the hundreds of private and public records which are searched and assembled. A report can be customized, depending upon the depth of detail necessary for the investigation. A simple report with credit header identifying information is often sufficient. An advanced report, including a multiple database search with telephone and utility records and financial information on bank accounts, stock ownership, and insurance policies, may be required in preparation for hardball negotiations or litigation.

Information from Proprietary Sources

Sometimes the information supplied by the databases is supplemented with additional information developed from proprietary sources such as contacts at the financial institutions or telephone companies. By the time the information from the databases has been merged and assembled, the report contains a complete picture of your personal and financial life with all of the details available for inspection and use—without your knowledge and outside of your control. Look-ups are a powerful source of information for investigators—often providing a comprehensive package of information to combine with the details available through the use of sources and pretext strategies.

The services offered by the look-ups are capable of such powerful and wide reaching searches that law enforcement agencies at each level rely heavily on these companies for assistance in their efforts. The look-ups are used to locate people suspected of criminal activity and to track down witnesses, friends, and associates of criminal suspects.

Computerized databases are among the most important weapons in the prosecution of financial crimes. According to the Federal Trade Commission Report to Congress, the Financial Crimes Enforcement Network (FinCEN), an arm of the U.S. Department of the Treasury, relies heavily on computerized databases to prevent and detect money laundering. FinCEN combines financial information reported by banks with a multiple database search from the look-ups and offers these intelligence reports to other federal and state agencies. The Secret Service and the National White Collar Crime Center of the Justice Department subscribe to more than a dozen look-up services and conduct searches for themselves and related agencies investigating economic crimes.

Summary

Recent advances in Internet and software technology create vast new capabilities for gathering and distributing private information. Diverse pieces of information, located in filing cabinets and warehouses, physically separated and apparently unrelated are digitalized, searched, and assembled into a single electronic profile.

The availability of this information may have certain legitimate benefits to both the government and the private sector. More information can lead to greater efficiency in law enforcement and tax administration. Commercial interests need information to supply credit, market goods and services, and combat fraudulent business practices.

But on a personal level unrestricted access to private information may cause a variety of realistic threats to an individual's psychological, financial, and physical well-being. Privacy intrusions are disturbing and distasteful to most people. In the course of our personal and business lives, we make many highly selective judgments about what we are willing to reveal about ourselves and to whom we wish to tell it. These decisions are important. Private information in the wrong hands can be damaging. We want to control who knows what about our lives for our safety and financial security.

The ability of strangers to access information about our personal financial assets seems to create the greatest sense of insult. The inability to control that flow of personal information—to not know who or why someone is looking at us—produces a profound sense of danger and anxiety. In the succeeding chapters, we will look at the actual dangers presented by these privacy intrusions, and then we will discuss the strategies that will successfully control those risks.

CHAPTER TWO

Who Needs
Financial Privacy

THE AVAILABILITY OF INFORMATION about your identity and your financial matters creates potential dangers from a variety of sources. The actual degree of threat to you may be high or low depending upon your business and personal circumstances. But we will give you some examples from our own experiences to help you measure the risks that you face.

The Lawsuit Threat

Increased access to financial information provided through the Internet and advanced search capabilities have smoothed the litigation process for every plaintiff's lawyer. The threshold issue of every lawsuit—*can this defendant pay up*—can now be resolved quickly and inexpensively. Until recently, it was not always so easy to determine this. As we discussed in the last chapter, real estate and bank accounts scattered around the country were difficult to locate in an asset search. A lawyer had to do a lot of digging and ask plenty of questions to make sure the potential defendant had enough money to make the case worthwhile. If there was any uncertainty about collecting the judgment, the lawsuit usually did not go forward. A lawyer would tell his prospective client, "Bring me some evidence that he has money, then I'll file the case." The process of gathering accurate information often took months or years, and the lawyer or the client might lose interest and move on to other things. A lack of reliable information slowed the speed of the litigation freight train.

But now the attorney can make a call to the investigator or can contact the look-up service directly to produce a comprehensive asset report on real estate holdings, financial accounts, and business ownership. Questions about whether a potential defendant can pay are now resolved quickly and efficiently.

A wealthy client, Allen, invested $10,000 in a software development business owned by a college acquaintance, Mark. Allen received two percent of the stock in the company, put away the certificates, and didn't think about it again for several years until one day he was served with the lawsuit. The suit alleged that the company had breached a contract to develop a particular program for a customer. The failure to deliver the program on time had cost the customer millions of dollars; it was now suing for $25 million. Allen was named as a defendant, together with the company which was primarily a service business with no substantial assets. It was clear that the real target in the case was Allen and not the company. Allen had $3 million of stocks and bonds in several brokerage accounts and this was the prize the plaintiff was after.

The case was disturbing. From a legal standpoint, Allen, as a minority shareholder—not even an officer or director—had no liability for any obligations of the company. Even if the damages were caused as alleged, Allen had no input or responsibility for the operations of the business.

The case had been filed solely because the other side had run an asset search on all of the shareholders—looking for a "shakedown" target—and they hit the jackpot when they found Allen's accounts. The attorney for the other side later admitted to us that if they hadn't found Allen's money, they wouldn't have filed the case. They had nobody else to go after. But now they had a perfect setup. Although Allen had no real liability, what happens in court is often different than what we think should happen.

As a named defendant in the case and the only one with money, Allen faced a difficult choice—fight or settle. If he fought, there was a risk that he could lose the lawsuit with damages of several million dollars plus attorney fees. That would probably wipe him out financially. If he won the case, it would still cost $100,000–$150,000 in legal fees and expenses and would absorb much of his time and emotions for at least the next few years. The lawyer for the other side knew how to play the game.

After several months of painful negotiations, Allen settled the case for $450,000. It was difficult for him to pay the money—mostly from an emotional standpoint—because he had done nothing wrong. But he was trapped and outmaneuvered, and he had no choice. By holding his money in an unprotected form, easily discovered and reachable, he was a vulnerable target. Once spotted, the sharks moved in for the kill and then it was too late.

This case provides a frightening example of the *"deep pocket"* litigation threat. Easy access to financial information allows unscrupulous plaintiffs and lawyers to legally extort money from unsuspecting and defenseless victims. Financial information is the fuel that ignites the lawsuit. The proper strategy is to hold your assets in a private and protected form, which cannot be discovered or reached by a potential adversary. Then you are no longer an attractive or vulnerable target for legal threats and attacks. When you block access to information about your bank accounts and real estate, you will discourage a potential lawsuit before it begins.

Celebrities Guard Their Privacy

Some of our first clients in the area of financial privacy were high profile celebrities in the sports and entertainment world. The common thread was that all of these clients had the primary objective of keeping secret the property they owned. This desire is understandable and legitimate. Our culture has an insatiable preoccupation with the private lives of celebrities. We want to know what they are doing, where they go, and who they go with. Celebrities attract attention, and much of it is unwanted and intrusive. Newspapers, magazines, and television shows both satisfy and stimulate the appetite of the audience for ever deeper and more intimate details of personal lives. The public disclosure of private matters is usually harmless but sometimes not. Too often information is made public—medical records, sexual indiscretions, and details of family life—which is embarrassing and damaging to personal relationships and reputations.

Celebrities and public figures always attempt to guard their privacy. They don't want their addresses and telephone numbers known, and they don't want the newspapers and television shows doing stories about what they own. Have you ever heard a story headlined "Details about Sylvester Stallone's $90 million bank account—Tonight at 11"? You will never hear that story because neither Stallone nor his advisors would ever open an account at a bank or brokerage firm with his name or Social Security number.

They would always use some form of Privacy Trust to hold the account so that ownership could not be traced to him.

A recent article in the *Wall Street Journal* was titled "The Rich and Famous Use Trusts to Hide Ownership: How Spielberg Just Did It." The story described how film director Steven Spielberg sold his Malibu, California home to special effects whiz Stanley Winston. The article reported that a trust was used by both buyer and seller for privacy purposes. The article noted that Spielberg is just one of a growing number of individuals using trusts as a strategy to protect the privacy of their home ownership. An East Hampton real estate broker was quoted: "I'm seeing it much more. A couple of years ago, one or two were purchased this way out here. It was really the exception, and now it's the rule." Other celebrities mentioned in the article using the trust strategy included Empress Farah Diba Pahlavi, widow of the Shah of Iran; Crown Prince Pavlos of Greece; Craig McCaw, billionaire cellular phone tycoon; and Paul Allen, cofounder of Microsoft.

According to First American Real Estate Solutions, a California real estate information company, twenty-nine houses in Beverly Hills were recorded in 1998 with the owners name listed as a trust, limited partnership, or corporation. Five years ago not a single transaction was recorded in this manner.

Sometimes, protecting private information from unwanted disclosure is a matter of personal safety. One of our clients, a well-known actress, owned five vacation homes in different parts of the country. The client held title to the properties in her name—a matter of public record and easily discoverable by anyone inclined to do so. It was important to her to conceal the ownership of these properties. There are simply too many unstable and dangerous individuals out there to make the addresses of her homes available to the public.

Other clients have different privacy needs. We represented a well-known financial columnist and television personality. He had achieved fame by correctly predicting the market crash of 1987 and had parlayed this lucky call (by his own admission) into frequent guest appearances on the nightly news, commenting about why the stock market went up or down on a particular day. He was a featured stock market analyst on a regular weekly television show about Wall Street. As a leading investment guru, his opinions about individual stocks and the market in general were widely followed (and believed) by the public. He made well over a million dollars a year by publishing a weekly newsletter with his investment advice.

Not surprisingly, when it came to managing his own portfolio, he was a terrible investor. He defied the odds by *losing money on almost every trade*—not easily accomplished in the relentlessly rising market of the 1990s. His investment portfolio lost money month after month in the biggest bull market in history. And the history of all those trades was recorded in his account statement, under his name and Social Security number at his brokerage firm. He was terrified that someone would gain access to information about the account and publicly disclose his trading results. That would be personally embarrassing as well as financially devastating. At a minimum, his credibility as an investment guru would be seriously tarnished if these facts were revealed to the public.

The solution was to create a Privacy Trust to conduct the investment activity. Arrangements were made so that the client could continue (if he wished) to manage and invest the account but the ownership was moved into the name of the trust. In chapter 10, we will discuss the details of how the Privacy Trust works. For now, the client's account, in the Privacy Trust, was identified at the brokerage firm with the name and federal tax identification number of the trust. There was no information on the account which would connect it in any way to the client. He was free to make all the bad investments he wanted—and the public would never know.

Those who are the subject of public attention work hard to craft a public image consistent with what they want to accomplish. Public relations specialists create a polished picture of the celebrity, which is then carefully managed and presented through the media. The distribution of information is controlled and is always packaged in the most favorable light. Information about what someone owns and details about money and bank accounts is never an appropriate topic for public discussion. There is no politician or public figure who would voluntarily reveal the intimate details of his or her financial life. Those who are sensitive to public disclosure of private information and who wish to control the financial information that can be accessed generally adopt strategies to create privacy for personal and financial matters.

Business Competitors

In the business world, success or failure often depends upon the quality of information held by each of the parties. Every business wants to know what their customers, vendors, employees, and competitors are up to. Is a competitor courting an important customer? Is your top manager thinking about leaving? Can you negotiate a lower price from your vendors? Companies gather information about each other hoping to create a strategic advantage. Corporation X, attempting to underbid Corporation Y, will employ a variety of legal and sometimes illegal tactics to find out how much Corporation Y will bid on a large contract.

The banking records of a company often contain valuable secrets which are dangerous in the wrong hands. Business checking accounts reveal the amounts paid to key employees, receipts from particular customers, marketing expenses, and every other detail of income and expense. Gross receipts and cash flow are apparent from an analysis of the account statements. A business competitor with this information knows how much to offer a key employee to "steal" him. He can see how much you pay your suppliers and how much the best customers are paying—and can offer them a better deal. He can determine the amount spent on marketing and advertising and the receipts generated from those dollars. In short, many of your most private business matters are revealed in your company's bank and financial records. An adversary in possession of those records poses a threat to the security of your business.

Pre-Divorce Planning

Much of the business of the private investigators comes from spouses engaged in pre-divorce planning. Savvy divorce lawyers will tell prospective clients to find out as much as possible as early as possible—before the papers are served. It is much easier, and ultimately more accurate, to gather evidence about financial assets beforehand, when the waters are relatively calm and before the other spouse has begun to think about issues such as hiding and protecting assets.

The plan, which is recommended by the attorney, involves a thorough asset search by a qualified private investigator. A report will be prepared listing real estate, business interests, and bank and brokerage account numbers with balances and transactions. These assets can then be identified and *frozen* at the time the divorce papers are filed. Once the divorce case is filed, money and property often begin to "move." When this happens, locating assets can become a messy and expensive task.

A recent *Business Week* article illustrated the difficulties a spouse can encounter tracking assets after the divorce litigation has begun. Two months before filing for divorce, Swiss industrialist Donald Hesse allegedly transferred $200 million of stock in Hess Holdings to an offshore trust in Gibraltar. Joanna, his American wife, has purportedly spent $600,000 in legal fees in numerous unsuccessful attempts to assert a claim on the funds.

In the book called *Tao of Divorce/A Woman's Guide to Winning*, divorce lawyers Steven L. Fuchs and Sharyn T. Sooho advise women to "win" the divorce battle with ancient Chinese tactics of strategic planning, stealth, and deception.

> *While still living in the marital home, you have a unique opportunity to acquire this information and to continue to maintain close physical proximity to your husband, his financial records, and his confidants. Sage Warriors can gain advantage by accessing strategic information during this window of opportunity we call the pre-filing, "planning stage."*

The authors advise women to perform thorough asset searches, photocopy important documents, monitor telephone calls, and build evidence of adultery, in secret, "while still living in the marital home."

It's not to clear to us exactly when this "planning " is supposed to start. How early in the marriage does the "Sage Warrior" begin to formulate her battle plan? Should she even wait to get married? Why not start on the first date with a little discrete photocopying—maybe a quick dash over to Kinko's on the way to the restroom?

Private investigators are experiencing a booming business in asset searches for strategic planning during all phases of a personal relationship. We have apparently reached the point where preparing for marriage includes a search by each side for the assets of the other to determine the necessity or accuracy of the prenuptial agreement. During marriage, staying informed means acquiring regularly updated asset reports and an analysis of phone records and credit card purchases. But when the marriage is over—is when the *real* action begins.

Ex-Spouses

Even after the divorce has been finalized and the marital property divided, one spouse often has an incentive to keep financial tabs on the other. Alimony payments, and even property settlement agreements, can be modified years after the divorce, based upon a change in the financial circumstances of one of the parties or upon newly discovered information.

A friend, Alex, was divorced and his wife, Liz, was awarded alimony of $400 per month for ten years. They had only modest assets at the time.

Starting immediately after the divorce, Liz had a private investigation firm perform annual financial "checkups" on Alex. Despite the divorce, she had confidence in his ability to make money— and she wanted to know about it when he did. Three years later, the investigator reported that Alex had indeed become successful. He had built his computer software business into a promising enterprise—worth more than $3 million.

Liz's faith in Alex had paid off. She consulted with her attorney, and they filed a petition to modify the divorce decree. She argued that based upon Alex's new wealth the amount of the alimony award should be increased. Also, she claimed that Alex's idea for his business had been developed during their marriage—the company stock was marital property and she was entitled to half.

Although it wasn't clear which argument he relied upon, the judge increased the alimony from $400 to $9,000 per month. He also awarded her $1.2 million in cash for a retroactive increase in prior alimony payments, her marital interest in the company stock, and attorneys' fees and court cost.

A client of ours, Dennis, was awarded custody of his two-year-old son Michael, following a divorce from his alcoholic and abusive wife, Marie. After the divorce Marie never contacted Dennis or visited with Michael. Luckily, Dennis was a good father and Michael developed into a smart and happy young boy. Dennis was a high school science teacher and over the years managed to save about $100,000 for Michael's college education.

One day, ten years after the divorce, Dennis received an unpleasant surprise—a telephone call from Marie. She said that she was getting her life together and wanted to contest custody of Michael. She also said that she had run an asset check on Dennis through a local investigation firm and had discovered the college savings account. Getting directly to the point of the call, she offered to give up her custody claim in exchange for a payment of the $100,000.

Unfortunately, the cat was out of the bag at that point, and there was nothing we could do (other than advise Dennis to call the police). So he paid her the money because he couldn't risk jeopardizing his life with his son.

It is a cliché by now to say that "information is power." But we can see that those who are skillful in acquiring the right information can successfully achieve objectives otherwise impossible to accomplish. Bargaining is about knowing the strengths and weaknesses of your opponent. A lawyer, business competitor, spouse, or ex-spouse with information about what you own can exploit this knowledge to attack your most vulnerable points.

Intimidation Tactics

It is not only the plaintiff's lawyers who use the services of investigation firms. Attorneys who are defending a case often turn to investigators to dig up as much dirt as they can on the plaintiff, his family members, and even the opposing lawyers.

An article in the *New York Times* by Nina Bernstein describes the frightening story of what happened to the plaintiffs in a lawsuit against oil giant Texaco arising out of a refinery explosion. According to the article, Texaco hired a private investigation firm to investigate those injured by the explosion and the attorneys who had filed a class action lawsuit on their behalf. "Through commercial databases unknown to most citizens, law enforcement computer files that are supposed to be off-limits to civilians, electronic surveillance equipment readily sold in spy shops, and simple telephone scams common in the information underground, Texaco's private eye quickly amassed sensitive knowledge about dozens of people involved in the explosion claims." This information was then used to threaten and intimidate some of the claimants into changing or fabricating testimony. One of the plaintiff's attorneys claimed that the investigator bugged his office, extorted false accusations against him, and engineered his indictment for an obscure insurance code violation. "By the time Mr. Buchanan was acquitted in March, his career and the remaining class action lawsuits were in shambles."

If you are involved in litigation, from the side of either the plaintiff or defendant, you are likely to face an adversary attempting to embarrass, intimidate, and harass you through the use of telephone and medical records, credit card and account information, interviews with neighbors, and extensive private data collected from investigation services. The ability to gather these extensive reports quickly and inexpensively through a network of databases ensures that these hardball legal tactics will dominate the litigation process into the future.

Criminal Threats

The availability of personal identifying information and financial information creates a variety of new dangers when used in connection with fraudulent or other unlawful activities.

A fast growing and popular crime is known as "identity theft." The perpetrator obtains the intended victim's name, Social Security number, and key identifying information from a look-up service, together with account numbers and balances. The thief can then obtain credit cards and purchase merchandise for credit—all under the victim's name. A Maryland couple stole the identity of hundreds of affluent individuals located through the Internet databases. They obtained birth certificates, driver's licenses, credit cards, and bank accounts and then stole more than $100,00 under the assumed identities before they were arrested and pled guilty. This type of fraud typically produces, for the unwitting victim, a nightmare of judgments, collection actions, and credit damage which may take years to repair.

Access to financial information can also produce extortion attempts through outright threats of violence. In one heavily reported, nearly unbelievable example, a prison contracted with an information vending service to supply inmate labor for data processing services. One inmate, a convicted rapist, used the personal information on the database to compose and send a threatening extortion letter to an Ohio grandmother. Others with criminal intent acquire information about potential victims by reviewing account information and business ownership. Organized crime now uses high tech database searches to locate potential extortion victims—targeting those with successful businesses or substantial accounts with threats of physical violence to an individual or a family member.

Discovering account information and the proper identifying information creates the opportunity to steal funds directly from bank accounts. Once the criminal has located an account with sufficient funds, he poses as the account owner and requests a cashier's check. The check can be directed to a new address or can be picked up in person. Experienced criminals know when a signature will be required and can plan accordingly. The cashier's check can be deposited in a newly opened account at a different institution using the victim's identity. As soon as allowable, the funds are transferred overseas or withdrawn in new cashier's checks. The victim is left to fight it out with the financial institution about whether it was he or someone else who withdrew the funds.

Telemarketing fraud targeting the elderly is facilitated with easy access to information services. For example, a search can be made for names, addresses, account numbers, and balances for individuals over eighty years of age. Posing as a bank employee, the telemarketer can offer a variety of phony but tantalizing investments. It's not difficult to trick the victim into authorizing a transfer of funds into the criminal's account. The eighty-five-year-old mother of a friend lost $65,000 to a scam artist posing as a bank employee offering a "guaranteed fifteen percent per year return." In these situations, with the victim himself authorizing the bank to move money from his account, there is generally no right to recover the stolen funds from the bank. A loss of retirement savings through this type of fraud can have devastating financial and personal consequences for the victim.

Laws Protecting
Financial Privacy

There is no comprehensive scheme of state or federal privacy protection for financial accounts or personal identity information. While many countries around the world have a long tradition of legal and constitutional protection for bank accounts and customer identity, the United States provides no such rights. Court decisions and legislation make it clear that a right to personal privacy does not extend to banking or financial records. All major legislation enacted over the last fifty years has been directed toward record keeping, reporting, and disclosure of financial transactions. Under existing federal laws, *banks and financial institutions are not prohibited from disclosing customer account information to third parties.*

For example, the disingenuously named Bank Secrecy Act of 1970 provides no bank secrecy protection whatsoever. In fact, it attempts to minimize secrecy by requiring that a bank obtain the correct identifying number of the customer for each account (not just interest bearing accounts) and imposes strict reporting requirements for cash transactions greater than $10,000. *Rather than restricting disclosure, the law imposes disclosure requirements in a variety of circumstances.*

In the 1976 case of *United States v. Miller,* the United States Supreme Court held that financial account records are business records belonging to the bank—not to the customer—and that the individual right of privacy does not protect disclosure of this information. The customer has no right to prevent the use of account records by the bank for whatever purposes it wishes. Following *Miller,* Congress passed the Right To Financial Privacy Act. Again, this is a grandiose and misleading title for legislation that does nothing to create or protect a right to financial privacy. Instead, it simply codifies government procedure for obtaining customer financial records from banking institutions.

In response to recent investigative articles in the *New York Times* and *Washington Post* detailing the availability of financial information from investigators and information brokers and the increasing public outrage over these privacy abuses, the Administration and Congress are now introducing measures attempting to tighten the flow of financial information. In August 1998, federal regulators warned the national banks to improve their security procedures and to take precautions against unauthorized disclosure of private customer information. The banks were told that current safeguards were "inadequate to protect customer privacy" and that they should impose stricter password and verification methods to improve security. In response to questions on this issue, Federal Reserve Chairman Alan Greenspan acknowledged that there is "uneven privacy protection" for financial information.

The House Banking Committee addressed the issue of financial privacy with hearings in July 1998. A long list of witnesses included Mozelle W. Thompson, chairman of the Federal Trade Commission; Julie L. Williams, acting comptroller of the Currency; and representatives of the American Bankers Association. They testified about rampant privacy abuses, unauthorized disclosure of customer information, and the need for additional security measures.

The legislation crafted in response to these serious issues is a bill known as the Financial Privacy Act of 1998. Unfortunately, the scope of the legislation is exceedingly narrow. It addresses only the limited practice of pretexting rather than the larger issue of unauthorized disclosure of account information by financial institutions. The proposed law would make it a federal crime, punishable by up to five years imprisonment, to obtain financial account information through fraudulent or deceptive techniques, including misrepresenting one's identity to a bank employee. The bill targets the investigators who rely on pretext to obtain personal account information, but it still allows financial institutions to continue to distribute and market sensitive customer information without restriction.

Although this legislation had not passed Congress at the time of this writing, it is likely that this bill or one similar will be enacted within the near future. However, it is doubtful that the passage of this type of legislation will have a significant impact on the problem. "Pretexting," the main target of the bill, is only one means of obtaining private information. Most account information is located through sources or is available from records at the financial institution.

Pretext is generally employed only by marginally legitimate investigators, at the fringe of their profession, with little training or access to more sophisticated resources. For those who rely on pretext, it is unlikely that the threat of criminal penalties will dampen the level of activity. Criminal penalties for drug violations and an army of enforcement personnel have made only the slightest dent in the narcotics trade. If legislation is passed which cracks down on this technique, some information brokers may alter the way they do business but it is unlikely that the flow of financial information will be diminished to any serious extent.

CHAPTER THREE

Searching for the Deep Pocket Defendant

The Litigation Explosion

IT HAS BEEN ESTIMATED that 50,000 lawsuits are filed in this country every day of the week. This has come to be known as the "litigation explosion." Whatever the causes—a breakdown of traditional values, the loss of a sense of community, too many hungry lawyers, wasteful insurance companies—the impact on each of us is significant.

When patients sue doctors, the cost of healthcare rises. To compensate for products liability claims, manufacturers add a premium to the price of their products. Litigation cripples business. It is time consuming, expensive, and emotionally charged. It detracts from our ability to focus on productive matters, as attention is directed away from matters of efficiency and innovation. Parties to a lawsuit spend so much time meeting with lawyers and fighting with the other side that nothing gets accomplished. As businesses are dragged under by the burdens of litigation, our whole society suffers.

If you are engaged in any business activity or if you have a professional practice, chances are that sooner or later you will be sued. And if you are sued, everything that you have worked hard to create will be placed in jeopardy. The costs of defending even a frivolous suit can easily reach $50,000 to $100,000. Once you get to court, you will find that the system is heavily weighted toward the sympathetic plaintiff, as judges and juries play Robin Hood with your money. These judges and juries are continually expanding theories of liability, and stratospheric damage and punitive damage awards are now routine. It is no longer uncommon for awards in negligence cases to exceed $1 million.

Our legal system should hold people responsible for their acts. If someone causes injury, that person should be required to fairly compensate the victim for his loss. Not many people would seriously object to this principle. The problem is that this general principle bears no relationship to what is actually occurring in the legal system today.

The Ability to Pay

The reality of our legal system is that people are named as defendants in lawsuits not because of their degree of fault but because of their ability to pay. When an attorney is approached by a potential client who is claiming injury or economic loss, the attorney will consider whether a theory of liability can be developed against a party who can pay a judgment. This is called the search for the "Deep Pocket Defendant."

The Deep Pocket Defendant will have substantial insurance coverage or significant personal assets. The measure of an attorney's skill is his ability to create a theory of liability which will connect a Deep Pocket Defendant to the facts of a particular case.

Here is an example of what might happen in a particular case. Mr. Woodrow is driving in his car. Mr. Fishbrain runs through a stop sign at an intersection, smashing into Woodrow's car and causing Woodrow severe injury.

From his hospital bed, Woodrow looks through the Yellow Pages and calls the first attorney he sees, the famous Alan Aardvark. He is what is known as a "contingent fee" lawyer. He works for a percentage of the ultimate recovery and determines whether to invest his time and money in a case based upon what his expected return will be. Since the time and expense of preparing for litigation can be considerable, an attorney cannot afford to take a case that is not likely to pay off. Remember—*no recovery, no fee.* Usually the attorney advances all costs and expenses, and in exchange, he recovers these costs plus 30 percent to 40 percent of any amounts which he can get from the defendant.

Before Aardvark decides to take Woodrow's case, he will want to do some serious research to determine the merits of the case. Not the legal merits—the financial ones. He will want to know whether Fishbrain has substantial assets in order to make the case worthwhile.

Aardvark runs a financial search and determines that Fishbrain has no insurance and no significant assets such as a home or a retirement nest egg. What happens? Is that the end of the case? As for Fishbrain, it probably is the end of the case. Aardvark is not going to waste his time suing someone who can't pay. But Aardvark is not going to give up so easily. He has a client with substantial injuries and that means a large damage award—big bucks. But first he has to find someone who can pay.

Here is how a good lawyer would analyze the case to try to draw in a Deep Pocket Defendant:

1. Was Fishbrain on an errand for his employer at the time of the crash? If so, the employer can be sued.

2. Did Fishbrain have any alcohol in his system? The restaurant that served him may have liability.

3. Was Fishbrain on any medication? The pharmacist, drug company, or physician may have potential liability for failure to provide proper warnings, or for writing or filling the prescription improperly.

4. The stop sign Fishbrain ran through was in a residential neighborhood in front of someone's house. Did the homeowner properly maintain his property and clear his foliage to provide an unobstructed view of the stop sign? If not, there is a case against the homeowner for negligence.

5. Did the municipality take due care in the placement of the stop sign? Should it have used a traffic light instead? There may be a case against the city or county.

6. The driver's side door of Woodward's car collapsed on impact. There is a possible case against the manufacturer for not making a more crash resistant frame.

Do you see how far we are moving away from Fishbrain—the person responsible for the accident—in an effort to tie in a remote Deep Pocket Defendant? In any rational legal system, Fishbrain would be regarded as the wrongdoer—he disobeyed the traffic law and he caused the injury. Instead, we have an attorney trying to force the blame onto someone else—who wasn't at the scene and doesn't even know the people involved.

The example that we just gave you is taken from a real case. Guess who ended up as the defendant.

In the actual case, the defendant was Fishbrain's ninety-two-year-old widowed great-aunt Ellen. As it turned out, she had purchased the car for Fishbrain as a gift to him. Aardvark's private investigator searched the assets of Fishbrain's relatives and found that Aunt Ellen had a house that she owned and some savings in the bank. She was named as the defendant in the case and was found liable on a theory called Negligent Entrustment. The jury found that she should not have bought the car for him. She should have known that he was a careless driver and might cause an accident. *She caused the accident by buying him the car.* The verdict was for $932,000, and Aunt Ellen lost nearly everything she owned.

The point of all this is that the foundation of every lawsuit is a defendant who can pay. Once such a defendant is located, it is easy enough to construct a theory of why that defendant should be responsible. Judges and juries often act on their emotions—not on the law. And when the contest is between an injured or a sympathetic plaintiff and a wealthy or *comparatively* wealthy defendant, the plaintiff will win virtually every time, regardless of the defendant's actual degree of fault.

As a result, the plaintiff's attorney will search for a party who can pay a hefty judgment. In the old days, it was said that " *He who has the gold makes the rules.*" Now the saying goes: " *He who has the gold pays the plaintiff.*" The fact is that no matter how remote your connection to an injury, if you have even modest assets, an attorney for the injured party will attempt to show that you are somehow legally at fault and you will be named as a defendant in the case.

Not Enough Good Cases
to Go Around

It used to be that people thought of Deep Pockets as a bank, insurance company, or other big company with billions of dollars to pay claims. Unfortunately, that's no longer the case. There are nearly 1 million lawyers now, and each year another 100,000 come out of law school and set up a practice. There are not enough good cases to go around.

A good case involves a serious injury with clear negligence by a company with significant assets or insurance. The problem for the lawyers is that most of the good cases go to a relatively small group of established trial lawyers with a history of multimillion dollar verdicts.

This makes sense. If you are seriously injured by an Exxon gasoline truck crashing into your house, you want the best trial lawyer you can find. You want a lawyer who has won large jury awards. The ability to argue successfully and convince a judge or jury of the merits of a claim is a unique and specialized talent. Few attorneys possess these skills, and those that do often earn millions of dollars each year. Since all contingency fee attorneys charge the same one third or 40 percent of the award, why not hire the best trial lawyer in the country? It doesn't cost you any more.

And if your case is a good one, any attorney would love to work for you. You can get the top trial lawyer in the country to handle your case, and he won't charge you a penny more than your niece's brother-in-law who has never been inside a courtroom. This is democracy in action. The poorest of the poor can hire the richest and smartest trial lawyer in the nation to fight for his rights. All it takes is serious injury or death and a defendant with deep pockets.

The Legal Extortion Racket

What are the rest of the lawyers going to do? What about the other 95 percent of trial lawyers who are not so great and not such good lawyers? How is a lawyer who is not at the top going to feed his family? His chances of getting your case against Exxon are about the same as hitting the lottery. Many of our close friends are personal injury attorneys. They think and dream about the one good case that will earn them enough to be on easy street. But the one good case never seems to come. Instead most lawyers make a living by looking for somebody to sue and filing bad cases with bad facts. As long as a lawyer can find a potential defendant with even modest assets, he will attempt to make his case. If he doesn't have a good case, he has to go with what he has. That's how he makes a living.

The lawyer is willing to gamble that by filing a case he will be able to squeeze a settlement or play "lawsuit roulette" with the jury. Just like the population in general, from whom they are drawn, jurors can be confused and misled by emotional and irrational arguments. Experiments in human behavior show that most of the time individuals are unable to distinguish the truth from a lie. When asked to distinguish truthful from untruthful testimony based upon the demeanor and expression of the witness, in a majority of cases, the subjects in the experiment incorrectly identified the lie as the truth and the truth as the lie. The conclusion of the study has frightening implications. *Jurors are more likely to believe a witness who is lying than one who is telling the truth.*

This phenomenon has been understood and exploited for years by political leaders and others with a message to sell. A lie which is repeated forcefully and with conviction becomes accepted as truth. Think of the Nazi propagandists and the McCarthy type demagogues who convinced millions of people of the truth of their cause. *Advertising messages repeated often enough are believed, regardless of the merits of the product and despite overwhelming evidence to the contrary.* That's the foundation of the multibillion dollar advertising industry and is the basis on which political leaders present their programs.

In the same manner, a lawyer attempts to "sell" his case to the jury. Facts are distorted. Lies, half truths, and perjured testimony are zealously advanced on behalf of the "injured" plaintiff. If things go right and the lawyer gets lucky or knows what he is doing, the jury will reward these efforts with a judgment for several hundred thousand or maybe a few million dollars. *Every day in court a sympathetic plaintiff prevails against a wealthy or comparatively wealthy defendant— even in those cases which appear to be absurd, illogical, and utterly without merit.*

Any lawyer who is still in business after a few years of practice has learned that the unpredictability of human behavior can be used to his advantage. The uncertainty of the outcome creates a potential risk of loss for even the most "innocent" defendant. Lawyers know that for most people the risk of financial loss also creates a highly uncomfortable level of emotional strain. If you have ever been sued—no matter what the cause—you understand that the unpredictability of the result and the possibility of economic loss can generate a severe degree of stress and emotional charge.

The Appeal of Settling

When a lawyer threatens to sue you, he is exploiting all of these facts about human nature. He knows that the outcome of the case will be uncertain regardless of the merit of the case. He knows that if you have reachable and collectible assets, the risk of loss will cause you extreme worry and stress. Finally, he knows that if you choose to fight the case, your time and your privacy will be violated and your resources will be depleted or exhausted by tens or hundreds of thousands of dollars in needless legal fees and costs. Doesn't settling the case sound much more appealing and logical?

Settling *is* more appealing, and that is exactly what you should do. As unfair as it sounds, if you fight the case, you may well lose. You will certainly spend much more money and time, and you may never recover from the emotional toll, the damage to your personal relationships, and the impact on your business.

If you have available and reachable assets which can be uncovered in an investigation, then the lawyers hold the leverage. They know that you are vulnerable, and you are better off settling the case. They want some easy money from you, and then they will move on to the next case. That's how the legal extortion racket works.

The Easy Cases Are Gone

Over the last few years, as the number of lawyers and lawsuits have increased, the insurance companies have adopted a policy of not settling cases. In the past, insurance companies routinely settled virtually every claim for a multiple of the injured party's medical expenses. A slip and fall or auto accident case was worth approximately six times the amount of the medical expenses incurred by the client.

When an individual went to an attorney claiming injury from an accident, the attorney would send the client to a cooperative doctor for extensive medical care and therapy. The doctors (and chiropractors) billed wildly for every imaginable treatment and procedure—almost all of which was unnecessary and was performed solely to inflate the amount of the medical bill. The physician would get paid out of the proceeds of the eventual settlement.

The lawyer had a nice fat medical bill—multiplied by six under the standard formula—which he could then present to the insurance company. The insurance company paid the inflated claim then raised the rates on all its policyholders to cover these costs.

At least several generations of personal injury attorneys and their doctor friends have made handsome livings by playing this game. But unfortunately for them, in most states, this game is over. Starting in the early 1990s, many insurance companies adopted a policy of no settlement. When the attorneys offered up the medical expenses, the claims adjusters were required by their companies to reject the claim. The policy was to litigate every claim all the way to trial.

It was understood that this strategy would be more expensive in the short run as the companies incurred huge legal bills fighting even the smallest claim. The upside was that the personal injury lawyers, deprived of their bread and butter fast settlements, would be driven out of business as their cash flow disappeared. Most attorneys can't wait two, three, or five years to get paid. And they certainly don't want to shell out all of the costs of bringing a case to trial, including depositions, expert witnesses, and discovery. Even worse is that after putting up all the money and going to trial, the case could be lost. Years of hard work and lots of money down the drain. That result means financial disaster and one more overeducated short order cook.

The insurance companies were like a pack of big goofy elephants. They had no idea that they had the power to step on and crush their lawyer adversaries. Once they decided to use their great strength—virtually unlimited capital—they were successful beyond their expectations. Lawyers stopped taking the "slip and falls," the bogus auto accidents, or any other insurance case without a big potential payoff. The insurance companies were the big winners.

The lawyers, their incomes and lifestyles seriously impaired, looked around for new groups to target—an easier and softer prey not so willing and able to fight back.

The New Deep Pockets

The new targets or the new Deep Pockets are those who have saved up some money for retirement, those who operate a successful business, and those who own a home or have some rental property with any equity. That describes a lot of people in our country. They are vulnerable because their savings are valuable to them. There are 100 million adults in the population, and 30 million have mutual funds, savings, or equity in their home. That's 30 million people with something valuable to lose, and 1 million lawyers who are aggressive and motivated. They want to move some of that money to their side of the table. One million lawyers file 19 million lawsuits each year, picking out the easy targets and causing great personal suffering and hardship.

The Fishbrains of the world don't get sued, and they don't have to spend their time, energy, and money defending a case. They don't get sued, because they don't have any money or anything worth taking. Aunt Ellen who bought him the car as a gift got sued because she had some money. *She* was the one who lost her home and all of her savings because *she* was the Deep Pocket. A lawyer's job is to tie a party who has some money into a case so that he will get paid. A good lawyer is one who can create a clever new theory of liability so that someone with money or insurance will be found legally responsible. Even if our common sense tells us that this Deep Pocket had nothing whatsoever to do with the injury, a judge or jury or court of appeals will decide a case based upon their own view of what is fair and rational.

A doctor prescribed antihistamines for a patient with an allergy. The patient ignored the warning label about driving while taking the medication and caused a serious auto accident. The patient had little insurance and few assets, so the doctor was sued. The plaintiff's lawyer successfully argued that the doctor *should have known* that the patient might drive his car while on the medication. The jury found the doctor liable for $6.2 million in compensatory damages. The doctor's malpractice insurance didn't pay a nickel of the claim since the policy only covered claims by a *patient*—not those injured by a patient.

Was the doctor really at fault here? He lost everything he owned, and he didn't do anything wrong. The mistake he made was not realizing that as a doctor, and as someone who had a home and some savings, he was an inviting and vulnerable target for a lawsuit. Holding his property in the traditional form with his wife, or in a living trust, put the doctor in jeopardy. The doctor did not see that he was an easy mark for a lawsuit.

Popular Deep Pocket Defendants

The Property Owner

Anyone who owns rental property is an excellent candidate for a lawsuit. In any measurement of potential liability, we would rank the property owner at the top of the list.

Let's assume you own a small apartment building. One evening a female tenant returns home from work and parks her car in the enclosed parking garage. As she gets out of her car, she is robbed by an assailant. Under these circumstances, you can expect a lawsuit against you as the owner of the property, for negligently failing to provide the proper level of security.

Regardless of the actual safety measures which you employ, the plaintiff's attorney will allege that you should have taken additional steps, such as installing video cameras, floodlights, or hiring security guards to protect the safety of the tenants. In essence, as a property owner and a Deep Pocket Defendant, you become a guarantor of the safety of your tenants, to the full extent of your available net worth.

■ A tenant was shot and killed in the alley behind the apartment building. It was found that the owner of the property should have provided better lighting for security in the alley. The jury awarded $27 million to the relatives of the tenant.

■ A fire in an apartment building killed one tenant and injured nine others. The owner had complied with all building code and safety requirements. He was sued for $5 million.

In these and similar cases, the owner of the property paid the claim or the judgment even though he had done nothing wrong. And that's where the problem lies. Under our current legal system, it doesn't matter whether you are really negligent or whether you do anything that is wrong. You can maintain your property in perfect physical condition, taking every imaginable safety precaution, and yet something can still go wrong. If a tenant is injured on the property—no matter the cause—it will still be your fault.

Having insurance on the property does not provide a guarantee that you will be free from personal exposure. Insurance is written with a long list of exclusions and exceptions. Insurance generally won't cover a lawsuit for undisclosed defects. Furthermore, it will be difficult to obtain an *amount* of insurance which is adequate to cover the full amount of the potential liability associated with injuries to multiple tenants. Even $1 million in coverage will not be sufficient if someone is seriously injured on your property. If several people are hurt in a fire or earthquake or other disaster, there may be $5 million–$25 million or more in potential damages.

Whatever amount is not covered by insurance will be your personal obligation. A judgment against you will be satisfied from your *personal assets* including your home, savings, and retirement funds. If something goes wrong at the property, everything you own can be lost. Any real estate—whether or not you have any equity in the property—represents an enormous source of liability to you and poses a danger to all other assets that you have accumulated.

Officers and Directors

Officers and directors of publicly traded companies are also popular Deep Pocket Defendants. All companies whose shares are publicly traded must file quarterly and annual reports with the Securities and Exchange Commission. These reports are known respectively as the 10–Q and 10–K filings. The purpose of these filings is to make information concerning the business and finances of the company publicly available. The law requires that public companies provide full disclosure of all material information which may influence the price of its stock.

A number of law firms employ young MBAs and attorneys to scrutinize each of the required filings made by these companies. If the stock of a company rises or falls sharply in response to some news item affecting the company, a law firm may attempt to show that the company's filings failed to adequately disclose certain material information. If any possible claim can be made, a class action lawsuit will be filed on behalf of current or former shareholders. The company, its officers, and its directors will be named in the suit. The defendants will fight the lawsuit or settle it, but in either event, the cost will be substantial and the only likely winners will be the lawyers who filed the action.

Physicians

All physicians are acutely sensitive to the risk of lawsuits. A recent study found that between 70 and 80 percent of all obstetricians had been sued, and the percentage of neurosurgeons and other medical specialists is equally as high. It seems that the public now perceives doctors, like auto mechanics, as capable of fixing any problem with the right tools and a good supply of parts. When these unreasonable expectations are not met—when a surgery or procedure is not successful—the patient and his family conclude that the only explanation is that the doctor must have been at fault. It is not fate, nature, or an act of God that is blamed for the misfortune. (It is much too difficult to collect a judgment from these parties.) As a result, many doctors have been forced to significantly narrow the scope of their practice to eliminate even modestly risky procedures. This type of defensive medicine inevitably drives up healthcare costs for everyone.

Real Estate Developers

Real estate developers and construction companies are another group with potentially significant personal liability. When a project is developed and sold, there may be liability to purchasers and subsequent purchasers for many years to come. Damages caused by latent (unseen) construction defects may be either uninsurable or may surface only after a policy has expired. As an example, California law states that a builder remains legally responsible for latent defects for up to ten years after the completion of the building. With potential liability having a "tail" of up to ten years, no builder is immune from a crippling lawsuit which may have been caused by the faulty workmanship of a subcontractor who has long since disappeared.

During periods when real estate prices are declining, lawsuits against developers and general contractors will be inevitable.

Homeowners who lose a significant amount of equity due to depressed market conditions often attempt to recover their investment by filing lawsuits, alleging construction defects against everyone involved in the project. That includes the geologists, engineers, architects, and the building tradespeople as well as the developer. These types of cases are enormously costly and time consuming to defend, and unless there is an insurance company involved to pay the costs, it is difficult for all but the largest companies to survive such lawsuits.

LIABILITY EVEN WHEN THE PATIENT IGNORES THE DOCTOR'S ORDERS

A recent segment on "60 Minutes" told the almost unbelievable tale of a psychiatrist and his former patient. The patient, a law student, had been acting unusually. He was referred to the student health service where the staff psychiatrist evaluated him. Over the course of several meetings, the psychiatrist diagnosed the patient as suffering from paranoid schizophrenia and prescribed anti-psychotic medication. The patient showed signs of improvement. The psychiatrist subsequently retired and instructed the patient to continue treatment with his successor on the psychiatry staff at the clinic. Eight months after last seeing the psychiatrist, and having never seen the successor, the patient stopped taking his anti-psychotic medication. His condition worsened. One day, during a delusional and psychotic episode, the patient shot and killed two people. As we would now expect, the patient sued the psychiatrist, claiming that the psychiatrist should have followed up and made the patient see the successor physician. At trial, the patient was awarded $500,000 against the psychiatrist whom he had not seen for eight months prior to the shooting and whose orders to follow up with medical care he ignored.

Another problem faced by developers is that each project requires a significant amount of cash, most of which is borrowed from a lending institution. The developer puts up the land as security and must also sign a personal guarantee for the entire amount. If the project is not successful, the developer must repay the loan out of his own pocket. As a result, one bad deal can wipe out many years of hard work.

Because of the high degree of lawsuit risk from these activities, the owners of these businesses are placing their entire net worth in jeopardy every single day. Each time a doctor performs surgery, he is literally betting the house on a successful outcome. Anytime something goes wrong, someone will sue. Every patient, client, or customer is a potential legal adversary.

Removing The Incentive To Sue You

The first goal of a sound business plan is to make your financial life private. We will discuss this in great detail in later chapters. For now, keep in mind that assets such as your home, your bank accounts, and your brokerage accounts can be moved into a properly designed plan. Someone wanting to see what you have will not find anything. Your real estate and your bank accounts won't be found when a lawyer or a private investigator searches for your assets.

Since the lawyer for a potential plaintiff will usually only sue you if he knows there are assets and he knows he will get paid, it is extremely unlikely that any lawyer would be willing to file a case against you. You can successfully discourage lawsuits by holding your property in a private and confidential manner, without revealing to the world what you own and how much you have. That's the first important objective that you can accomplish. The importance of privacy and asset protection will be emphasized as we present this material.

CHAPTER FOUR

What Happens in a Lawsuit

IN THIS CHAPTER we will discuss what happens in a typical lawsuit. We will go through the various stages of a lawsuit using a hypothetical case involving a fictitious Mr. John Williams.

Williams is an author who recently completed a detailed investigative study of a particular religious sect. After the book was published, the leader of the sect filed a lawsuit against Williams for defamation. The sect has a reputation for attempting to intimidate and coerce anyone who might reveal damaging information about the group, and the major weapon in this intimidation process is the use of lawsuits. (That is why we are not mentioning the group's name.)

A lawsuit has five separate stages:

1. Economic analysis of the case.

2. The pleadings.

3. Discovery.

4. Trial.

5. Collection.

Economic Analysis: Are You Worth Suing?

Before any lawsuit is commenced, the claimant (or plaintiff) and his attorney will review the economics of the case. The plaintiff will weigh the costs of prosecuting the case against the likelihood of victory and the amount of the probable recovery.

In our example, the financial investigation of John Williams revealed that he owned a home with about $100,000 of equity, a savings account at a bank with $65,000, and a brokerage account with $135,000 of securities. The decision was made to file the lawsuit. Here's how the plaintiff arrived at that decision.

Plaintiff's Cost to Sue You

Hourly Attorney

The costs involved in suing someone depend primarily on whether the attorney is working on an hourly rate or a contingency fee. Most, but not all, cases concerning business disputes are handled on an hourly basis. Typically, these hourly fees range from $100 to $375 per hour. Legal fees in pursuing a garden variety case to trial can be $50,000 to $100,000. In a case of some complexity, the legal fees can easily reach $1 million.

An hourly fee attorney has an economic stake in encouraging the litigation. Since the attorney gets paid his hourly rate, regardless of the outcome, there is a huge incentive for the attorney to "sell" the case to his client. The lawyer will encourage the client to sue in order to generate substantial fees for himself. (The next time you are encouraged by an hourly fee attorney to file a lawsuit, try asking him if he will take the case on a contingency.)

The attorney's inherent incentive to litigate discourages early reasonable settlements between the parties. We have seen again and again in our practice that it is nearly impossible to get an hourly attorney to devote his attention to an early and reasonable settlement. Instead, the lawyers generally adopt severe and inflexible negotiating positions while attempting to persuade the client that the *other* side is unreasonable. Cases are usually not settled early in the process unless the client is particularly sophisticated and understands his attorney's financial interest in pursuing the litigation.

If the case is not settled early, it is almost always settled late— when the client's resources or patience (or both) are nearly exhausted. Usually this occurs just prior to trial—*after* the client has already spent substantial sums and he finds out what the additional fees will be if a trial is necessary. At this point, the attorneys for both sides become reasonable in their demands. Whatever it takes, a settlement is reached at this point. That is why only about 1 percent of all the lawsuits that are filed ever get to trial.

Several years ago we represented a well-known professional athlete in a case against his former financial advisor. The financial advisor "sold" our client on a real estate investment by seriously misrepresenting the important facts about the deal. Our client had lost $100,000 and wanted his money back.

The other side (let's call him Mr. Jones) was represented by a large prestigious West Coast law firm. The firm was being paid on an hourly basis, $200 per hour, and we were working on contingency. We made a demand for $100,000, and the attorney for Mr.

Jones offered zero. Despite the fact that we had all of the evidence on our side and we stood an excellent chance of winning, the other attorney would not budge.

Prior to filing the lawsuit and over a period of several months, we kept talking but no progress was made. We were puzzled. Mr. Jones had a large and supposedly reputable company which handled investments for many entertainers and athletes. If we filed our suit, the negative publicity would certainly injure Mr. Jones' business and reputation. Once we filed our suit, surely all the other investors would also sue. It did not make any business sense for Mr. Jones to attempt to defend his unwinnable position.

At last, we concluded that Mr. Jones simply did not grasp his legal position. We were sure that his attorneys were telling him that he had a great case and he should not settle. We figured that he had probably spent close to $35,000 in legal fees at this point. His attorneys were milking him, and we were forbidden by the legal rules of ethics from speaking directly to Mr. Jones to let him know what was going on.

We finally decided that the only way to get to Mr. Jones was to get some independent third party to talk some sense into him. We suggested to Mr. Jones' lawyer that we mediate the case with a well respected former judge. Each side would tell its story, and the mediator would evaluate our claims. To our surprise, Mr. Jones' lawyer agreed.

Several weeks later, we had our mediation. Attorneys for both sides were present along with our clients. We each informally presented our case and then the judge turned to Mr. Jones and said: "I have been a judge for many years, and based on my experience I will tell you that, if you go to trial, you will lose. I don't know what your attorneys have been telling you, but I suggest you settle this case right now."

Apparently this little speech did the trick. Within a week we had our client's $100,000 back plus interest of $30,000. That was more than we had asked for originally. Mr. Jones also paid about $65,000 in legal fees in addition to the settlement amount, so it ended up costing him $195,000 instead of the $100,000 we had been willing to take on day one.

This story is not uncommon. It is the rule. Every plaintiff's personal injury attorney who deals with insurance companies knows that once the case is in the hands of an outside insurance defense legal firm, no settlement will be possible until right before trial. Attorneys on an hourly fee basis will prolong the case for as long as possible.

Expenses of Litigation

It is not just the attorney's fees that have to be calculated in determining whether to sue. The expenses of litigation must also be considered.

Everything connected with litigation seems to cost much more than it should. Fees to stenographers for a six-hour deposition are usually $1,000–$1,500. Nobody can figure out why it costs that much. When all of the costs of Discovery, travel, expert witnesses, filing fees, research, private investigators, and jury fees are added up, the amount will be mind boggling. A normal range for expenses will be $15,000 to $75,000 in a case of modest complexity.

Contingency Fees

Contingency fee attorneys do not charge by the hour. Instead, their fee is a specified percentage of any recovery. This amount is usually 33⅓ percent if the case is settled before trial and 40 percent if a trial is necessary. Since it is only large companies and very wealthy individuals who can afford to pay trial attorneys on an hourly basis, most lawsuits are handled on a contingency fee basis.

Usually the attorney agrees to advance all of the expenses and is repaid out of the recovery, if there is one. Although in most states the client is technically responsible for repaying expenses advanced by the attorney, it is rare that the attorney actually seeks to collect these amounts from his client. If there is no recovery, advances for costs are written off.

As opposed to hourly fee attorneys, who make money regardless of the outcome, the contingency fee attorney essentially bears all of the economic risk of the litigation. As we have seen, this risk and the potential reward can be quite substantial.

In this sense, the contingency fee attorney is an entrepreneur. The attorney, rather than the client, must carefully evaluate the merits of a particular claim. The potential recovery is balanced against the amount of work which will be required. A fast settlement of marginal claims is essential to the plaintiff's lawyer. He simply cannot stay in business advancing costs and spending time on small cases.

On cases with potentially large damage awards, the plaintiff's attorney is willing to carry the case to trial. Usually, he would prefer a fast settlement, but if he does not receive a satisfactory settlement offer, he will go to trial. Many of these attorneys are really gamblers at heart, and they are willing to invest a lot of time and money for a sizable payoff. And to get this payoff, *the most important element of the case is finding a defendant who can pay.*

■ The Search for the Big Bucks

Contingency fee attorneys love to have insurance companies, financial institutions, or large businesses as the defendant. If he wins, the attorney knows that he will collect, unless the amount of the judgment or the number of the claims causes the defendant to file for bankruptcy. That is what happened to A. H. Robbins (IUD) and the Manville Corp. (asbestos). They each filed for bankruptcy to halt the flood of litigation over their products. But ordinarily, these type of companies make good defendants.

If a potential defendant is an individual or a small company, the plaintiff's attorney is going to do substantial investigation before he commits his time and his resources to the case. There is nothing that attorneys like less than working on a case without getting paid.

You must assume then, that the attorney interested in suing you will perform a thorough financial investigation of your background, assets, and income. This work will usually be done by one of the many private investigation firms that operate in each city. The investigator usually subscribes to one or more of the database services offered by the individual reference services. A personal information report is compiled based upon the database search and the proprietary sources used by the investigator. The report may contain basic asset information including real estate ownership and financial accounts.

If you are one of many potential defendants in a case, the lawyer may not want to spend a lot of money on your investigation until he knows whether or not you are a worthwhile target. The first round of searches may be intended to narrow the list of potential defendants. Those who don't have a satisfactory amount of assets don't make the cut. They don't qualify for the all important second round—which usually involves getting sued.

If assets are located in the initial search, then a more detailed investigation is commenced with a view towards the litigation. As we saw in chapter 1, the search is accomplished quickly and for a modest fee. Financial assets are scrutinized to verify ownership, equity, and value. The investigator checks into outstanding liens and judgments to make sure that nobody else has a prior claim. Information from civil and criminal court cases, employment information, and income data may be gathered and presented to the attorney at this point to be analyzed in order to assess your merits as a defendant in the case.

The lawyer's favorite dilemma is when there is a large group of potential defendants—all with significant assets. Then the response is to name everybody. This often happens in medical malpractice cases. The hospital—together with every physician at the hospital who has any money—will be named in the lawsuit. Actual responsibility can be sorted out later—during discovery or at trial.

The financial investigation will produce one of three results:

■ **Substantial, relatively reachable assets are located.** The decision will be made to file the lawsuit.

■ **Insufficient assets are located to provide a worthwhile recovery.** The lawsuit will not be filed.

■ **No asset information is discovered one way or another.** This is a rare occurrence, but it happens. Since the attorney cannot develop a level of confidence that sufficient assets exist to pay a judgment, in all likelihood the case will not be commenced.

If the attorney is acting on an hourly basis rather than a contingency, the issue of collectability is a problem for the client but not the lawyer, since the lawyer expects to get paid regardless of the outcome. In most cases, any mentally sound, well-advised plaintiff will have his attorney perform a financial investigation of the defendant, prior to incurring substantial expenses in the case. If insufficient assets are discovered, only the most self-destructive client would elect to proceed with the case.

Defendant's Costs

If you are in the unfortunate position of being a defendant in a lawsuit, your lawyer will charge you on an hourly basis. No lawyers *defend* cases on a contingency arrangement. Like the lawyer representing the plaintiff on a time spent basis, you will be obligated to pay him whether you win or lose. What's more, your lawyer will undoubtedly require that you deposit a retainer to cover his anticipated expenses and costs as well. If you are a wealthy or seemingly wealthy person, your lawyer may tend to view you as a "meal ticket." And, come to think of it, *that is exactly what you are.*

The Pleadings Stage
The Nightmare Begins

The initial pleading in a case is the "Complaint" which is prepared on behalf of the plaintiff and sets forth the allegations of the defendant's wrongdoing. The Complaint is filed in the appropriate local court, and this filing commences the lawsuit.

In the usual case, the Complaint is produced by the plaintiff's attorney from one of a number of standard forms relating to the particular subject matter of the lawsuit. It is not necessary that the Complaint set forth anything other than the vaguest allegations of wrongdoing. The material facts are left to be uncovered during the Discovery process.

In our case, John Williams first learned that he was being sued when the Complaint and a Summons were served on him by a process server. In reading it, Williams saw that he was being sued for defamation by the religious sect. It alleged that Williams willfully and maliciously printed false statements about the group and asked for actual damages of $100,000 and punitive damages of $5 million.

Of course, Williams was distraught. He had known that the leaders of the sect would be angry about the publication of his book, but because he had been truthful and accurate in his reporting, he had not believed that there would be any grounds for a lawsuit. Now he knew that, groundless or not, he would have to incur substantial expenses in defending the lawsuit and that a considerable amount of his resources and time would be consumed in the process.

A friend of Williams referred him to a local lawyer who agreed to represent him in the defense. The attorney informed Williams that he would have to file a response (or "Answer") to the Complaint within thirty days and after that, the Discovery phase of the lawsuit would begin. He advised Williams that the costs of the defense could not accurately be estimated but a good guess was somewhere between $25,000 and $75,000. Williams paid his attorney a $15,000 retainer fee. Within the proper time period, the Answer was filed denying each and every allegation.

Pre-Judgment Attachments

A powerful weapon in the hands of the plaintiff's attorney is the Pre-Judgment Writ of Attachment. This remedy is used to freeze the assets of the defendant and place them under court protection prior to a judgment. This procedure is used to prevent the defendant from transferring, hiding, or wasting his assets before the plaintiff has a chance to collect. Cash held in a savings or checking account cannot be reached by the defendant once a Pre-Judgment Writ of Attachment has been issued. Similarly, real estate cannot be sold or refinanced.

A Pre-Judgment Writ can only be issued in certain types of cases. In California, it is available only in contract cases arising from a commercial transaction. It is not available against a defendant in a negligence suit. The plaintiff's claim must be for a specific dollar amount, and he must demonstrate a substantial likelihood that he will win at trial.

If a Pre-Judgment Writ is granted by the court, enumerated assets which are owned by the defendant are effectively frozen. As a result, the defendant may be unable to obtain working capital to carry on his business. And unless he has a source of funds unknown to the plaintiff, the issuance of the Writ can force the defendant to accept a fast and unfavorable settlement.

In our example, the plaintiff's claim against Williams did not arise out of a contract or a commercial transaction. The Writ was, therefore, not available to the plaintiff.

Discovery

Burying the Opposition

The Discovery phase of a lawsuit allows each side to probe the other side for facts as well as legal theories that might be helpful to build one's case and further elucidate the other side's trial strategy. Information is obtained from the opposing party by means of written questions (or "interrogatories"), face-to-face interrogation (called "oral depositions" or "examinations before trial"), and requests for the production of documents.

This is the stage of a lawsuit where one party may attempt to "bury" the opponent in paperwork. Typically, the side with the greatest financial resources now attempts to burden the other side to the greatest extent possible, in order to exhaust the opponents' financial resources. This can be accomplished by lengthy and numerous interrogatories, depositions, and subpoenas of documents, all of which are designed to cause the opponent to incur needless legal fees, embarrassment, expenses, and the greatest amount of overall aggravation.

It is a customary tactic in Discovery to attempt to uncover those intimate and personal details about the defendant's life and habits that he would not wish to have revealed in a public trial. The objective of the opposing attorney is to gather as much "dirt" as possible, with the hope of increasing his bargaining position in the settlement negotiations prior to trial.

Often, medical and psychiatric evaluations are permitted, including blood and urine testing to search for evidence of drug use or illness. Lawyers are permitted extraordinary leeway in the ostensible search for items that may have even the most remote relevance to the underlying case.

Searching Your Computer

A powerful discovery strategy is to subpoena the computer records of the other side. These records often provide the most direct and convenient path to all of the defendant's personal matters.

Lawyers now routinely demand to search computer and e-mail files in every case—often finding the "smoking gun" document that wins the case. Federal and state government agencies typically begin their investigations with a raid and seizure of written files and all computers. In the pending Justice Department antitrust litigation against Microsoft, internal e-mail messages to subordinates from Bill Gates about tactics for dealing with competitors is crucial evidence in the government's case.

Many people mistakenly believe that "deleting" a sensitive file will remove it from the computer. In fact, deleting sensitive files doesn't work. *When you attempt to delete a file or an e-mail message, the contents remain on the computer's hard drive, stored in its memory.* You can't see the file so you may think it's gone—but it's not. The "delete" function on your computer removes only the *name* of the file from the file listings in the computer directory—but the contents of the file itself are not altered or destroyed. The information is right there for anyone to look at—if they know some of the basic techniques.

Washington Mutual, the giant financial services firm, learned this lesson the hard way. According to a story in the *Seattle Times*, the company is attempting to recover a dozen computers it previously sold as surplus after learning that "deleted" Social Security numbers, loan applications, and job histories for an unknown number of customers—remain stored on the computer hard drives. The employee responsible for discarding the computers thought that the "delete" function would remove the information from the computers. The result of this mishap is an embarrassing public security lapse for the bank and a dangerous privacy breach for the customers.

If your computer is seized during litigation, the stored files and e-mail messages will be examined and searched to uncover incriminating evidence. Experts known as computer forensic technicians specialize in locating and recovering information from files which have been altered, deleted, or even partially destroyed. The information discovered in your computer's memory may provide a deadly accurate road map through your private financial and business matters.

A computer forensic firm gives this example in their brochure: "It was a messy divorce. The husband claimed he didn't have any savings or investments other than the ones he had disclosed... After processing his computer at our lab, we found the evidence we needed in cyberspace. The husband had been tracking his stocks via an online service and downloading the information into his financial program. Need we say more?"

The information stored in computer memory presents a unique challenge in litigation. Written documents, subpoenaed in a case, can be carefully reviewed before being delivered to the other side. The party producing the documents knows what's there and can prepare accordingly. It is also a fact that, although it is illegal to do so, incriminating documents are often removed or altered by the attorneys or the clients—before they are turned over to the other side. As a consequence, it is rare when damaging written information is voluntarily produced.

In contrast to written documents, you generally don't know and can't find all of the items stored in the memory of your computer. You may have letters, e-mail messages, financial records, personal notes, telephone numbers, and calendars—forgotten and invisible to you—but easily recovered by the forensics experts. If you are sued, the plaintiff will immediately attempt to get a court order prohibiting you from altering or removing any computer records. He will then copy the contents of the hard drive and search for incriminating—or at least embarrassing—material. You may have no idea what he will find on your computer, and so you can't control the information which is produced.

Of course, you will use the same tactics on the plaintiff. Your experts will look through all of his e-mail and note the Web sites he visited and the information that he tried unsuccessfully to "delete." The outcome of the dispute will often be decided based on which side *inadvertently* produces the most damaging evidence.

Shortly after filing the Answer, Williams was served with more than 100 pages of interrogatories with questions concerning nearly every detail of his life. He was also required to submit to five days of depositions during which time he was questioned by the attorneys for the religious sect. He was ordered to produce all personal computers from his home and office. All of the written notes which Williams had made in preparation for writing the book, including notes from his conversations with various confidential sources were subpoenaed and ordered to be turned over by the court. Many of Williams' family and friends were also subjected to extensive interrogation on the dubious grounds that they possessed some information which might possibly be relevant to the case.

Trial

By the time the case was ready to go to trial, four years after the original Complaint was filed, Williams had paid his attorney $85,000 and his attorney estimated that the cost of the trial might exceed an additional $50,000. Williams' attorney was approached by the plaintiff's counsel, who offered to settle the case, if Williams would pay the religious sect $35,000. Since this amount was less than the cost of the trial and less than the amount that Williams stood to lose if there had been a judgment against him, Williams accepted the offer and settled the case for the amount proposed. By accepting this proposal, he managed to save his house and still had nearly $85,000 in his savings account. The religious sect had proposed the settlement, because it really did not wish to go to trial and possibly lose the case with the resulting negative publicity. Instead, the sect believed that it had accomplished its dual objective of punishing Williams and discouraging future journalistic attempts to reveal information about the sect. In reality, it was an abuse of the legal process that was both the means and the end.

Had Williams gone to trial and won, he would not have been entitled to recover his legal fees and costs. In the United States, each party to a lawsuit is required to pay his own costs and expenses. This is known as the "American Rule." In some other countries, such as England and Japan, the prevailing party is entitled to recover its attorney's fees. The exception to the American Rule is that parties to a contract may specify in the agreement that in the event of a dispute, the prevailing party is entitled to recover any costs incurred in a lawsuit, including legal fees. But unless that "attorney's fees" provision is included in a contract, each side bears its own expenses.

Concern about legal fees and costs are usually only one component in the defendant's willingness to settle a case before trial. A second and perhaps more compelling influence is that the outcome of a trial can never be predicted. No one knows which facts will be important and whose testimony will be believed. A sympathetic or attractive plaintiff or a skillful attorney will often sway the emotions of the jury despite a complete lack of merit to the case.

The ultimate amount of the damage award also cannot be predicted with any level of confidence. One of our clients, a successful business owner, told us that he had previously been sued by a former employee on a completely outrageous and frivolous claim. Prior to trial, he turned down an offer to settle the case for $25,000, refusing to pay what he felt was pure "extortion" money. You can imagine his surprise when the jury awarded the plaintiff $750,000— based entirely on manufactured and perjured testimony.

Collecting Your Assets

The Wolf at Your Door

If Williams had lost the trial, the case would have then moved on to the collection stage of the lawsuit. Let's assume that there had been a judgment against Williams in the amount of $300,000. He could appeal the judgment to a higher court, but he would be required to post a security bond equal to the amount of the judgment.

This is an important concept to grasp. We have all been taught that in our system of justice, erroneous rulings by trial court judges, often political insiders with little trial experience themselves, will be scrutinized and reversed, if necessary, by more highly qualified appellate court jurists. But, in reality, the right to appeal seldom works well. To appeal, Williams would have to obtain the appeal bond through a licensed bonding company that would require him to post security equal to the $300,000 bond. That usually means posting property with a far greater value than that so that a sale of the property, if required, would net the bondsman $300,000.

Then there is the matter of the bondsman's fee—usually 10 percent of the bond, or $30,000 cash to Williams. This is all just for the privilege of filing an appeal. To have the appeal heard, Williams will have to pay for trial transcripts and retain an appellate lawyer who will charge him another $25,000 to $50,000 in most cases. During the time that the case is on appeal, the judgment creditor would not be permitted to take any steps to collect on the judgment. After the appeals were exhausted, the judgment creditor would then begin the collection process.

What all of this means for Williams, or any other litigant, is that taking one's right to appeal into consideration when evaluating a case is a bad strategic move. Appeals are fine for large corporations that have the financial ability to pay for them, or for criminal defendants, for whom they are free. For individuals entangled in the lawsuit process, the right to appeal is an illusory consolation.

Locating the Debtor's Assets

The collections process itself often begins with a procedure known as the debtor's examination. As stated, during the Discovery phase of the lawsuit, the plaintiff is generally prohibited from obtaining information concerning the defendant's assets. Typically, this information is not considered to be relevant to the underlying case and no Discovery with regard to the defendant's assets is permitted.

After judgment, however, location of the debtor's assets becomes the focus of the investigation. The debtor's exam may be presented by written questions or by oral examination. In either case, the debtor will be asked to list and describe all of his assets and to provide all banking records. He will also be asked whether he has made any transfers of any property by gift prior to or during the lawsuit. All of these questions are asked under oath, and the failure to provide true and complete answers is a felony.

The procedure for enforcing judgments and collection by a judgment creditor is established by the laws of each state. For our example, we will assume that our debtor, John Williams, is a resident of California. Although each state has a different procedure, there is enough similarity in concept to provide you with a general understanding of the collection process.

Personal Property

When a judgment has been entered, the court issues a Writ of Execution, which is essentially an authorization for the collection action. The judgment creditor gives the Writ of Execution to the marshal (or sheriff) with written instructions describing the property to be seized. The marshal is authorized to take possession of your property by removing it to a place of safe keeping or otherwise taking control over it. Property seized in this manner may then be sold at a public sale.

If your property is in the hands of a third party, the marshal directs that party to turn over the property. Your bank accounts and brokerage accounts can be seized in this manner. If a third party owes you money, that person is notified that he must make payment directly to the marshal's office.

Real Estate

The collection procedure for your real estate begins with the filing of a summary of the judgment ("Abstract of Judgment") with the county recorder in each county where you own property. The Abstract of Judgment creates a lien on the property, similar to a mortgage or deed of trust. The creditor does not have to designate the address of the property or, for that matter, must he even know in advance that you own any real estate in that location. The lien applies to any real estate which you own in that county and also applies to any real estate which you purchase in the future.

Once this Abstract has been filed, your property cannot be sold or refinanced without satisfying the judgment. You cannot avoid this lien by transferring the property to a third party. The lien remains attached to the property until the judgment is satisfied or expires. In California, judgment liens are in effect for ten years and can then be renewed for another ten years.

If the creditor does not want to wait for a voluntary sale or refinancing, he may file a Writ of Execution with the county recorder. After giving proper notice to you, the property is then sold to the highest bidder at a public sale. Cash from the sale is applied to the amount of the judgment, including interest and expenses of collection. Any surplus is returned to you.

Real estate which is sold at this type of public auction rarely brings in an amount greater than 50–60 percent of the actual value of the property. As a result, if there is a $100,000 judgment against you, a creditor may seize and liquidate $200,000 of your property before the debt and the costs are satisfied. The judgment of $100,000 just cost you $200,000, not including your legal fees and costs.

What You Can Save

With an aim toward avoiding the complete impoverishment of a debtor, the law provides certain partial or complete exemptions from the sale of certain property by a creditor for the collection of his judgment. For purposes of illustration, the following is an incomplete list of exempt property under California law:

◼ Government Benefits

Unemployment benefits, disability and health payments, and benefits under the Workers' Compensation law are exempt from collection.

◼ Life Insurance

State laws vary considerably on whether any or all of the cash value of insurance policies is subject to collection by a creditor. California exempts up to $4,000 in cash value as well as life insurance proceeds, which are reasonably necessary for the support of the debtor's family. In Texas and Pennsylvania, insurance annuities are entirely exempt.

■ Wages

Each state provides for a different degree of exemption of wages from garnishment. Garnishment is the procedure whereby a debtor's employer is directed to withhold some portion of the debtor's salary. The amount withheld is then turned over directly to the creditor. In California, up to 75 percent of the debtor's disposable earnings are exempt from garnishment.

■ Household Furnishings and Automobiles

Ordinary and necessary household furnishings, apparel, appliances, and other personal effects at the debtor's residence are exempt. Items having extraordinary value, such as antiques, musical instruments, or art work, are subject to execution. The debtor is entitled to proceeds from the sale of these items in an amount necessary to purchase a replacement of ordinary value. Automobiles for personal use are exempt up to $1,200.

■ Personal Residences

The personal residence of a debtor may be partially protected by the filing of a Homestead Exemption for a dwelling in which the debtor resides. In California, the amount of the exemption ranges from $50,000 to $100,000 depending upon whether family members are living at the residence and whether the debtor is over sixty-five years of age.

Some states have particularly liberal Homestead Exemptions. Florida allows a Homestead of ½ acre for urban property and 160 acres for property in rural areas. Texas provides protection for one acre of urban land and up to 200 acres for rural property. In

Massachusetts, the exemption is $100,000 for a family residence and $150,000 for a disabled individual over age of sixty-five.

■ Retirement Plans

IRA and Keogh plans are granted an exemption to the extent of reasonable support needs. Corporate pension and profit sharing plans, formed under ERISA, are fully exempt from judgment creditors.

■ Business Property

Property used in the business or profession in which the debtor earns his living is exempt to the extent of $2,500 of equity. The exemption applies to tools, books, equipment, one commercial vehicle, and other personal property.

■ Interests in Trusts

In most states, if a trust provides that a beneficiary's interest cannot be transferred, the interest is exempt from execution, until the amount is actually paid to the beneficiary. Also, if a trust requires the trustee to pay income or principal for the support or education of a beneficiary, these amounts are not reachable, until paid.

You can see from this discussion that unless you live in a state, such as Florida or Texas, which provides a significant homestead exemption, a lawsuit has the potential to obliterate virtually everything that you own. With this sobering thought in mind, let's look at the privacy and asset protection strategies which are designed to discourage these lawsuits and protect against future claims.

CHAPTER FIVE

Privacy and Protection With Corporations

A GOOD PLACE TO BEGIN our discussion of asset protection and privacy strategies is with the corporation—a familiar but often misunderstood planning tool. In this chapter, we will examine the advantages and disadvantages of a corporation and see how it fits in with the overall plan we will develop.

Corporations are a form of business organization permitted by law in every state. A unique feature of a corporation is that it issues shares of stock. A share of stock entitles a shareholder to vote on the election of a board of directors, which is charged with the overall management of the corporation. The board of directors elects the officers—the president, secretary, and treasurer, who are authorized to conduct the day to day business of the corporation. Many states permit a single individual to serve as sole director and to hold all of the corporate offices.

One of the unique features of a corporation is that it is intended to have a perpetual existence. The death of an individual director or officer does not terminate the existence of the corporation. Instead, the corporation carries on indefinitely until it is dissolved by a vote of the shareholders.

A corporation is legally formed and begins its existence upon the filing of Articles of Incorporation with the Secretary of State of the state of incorporation. You can choose to incorporate in any state you wish. It is not necessary to incorporate in the state where your business is located. A disproportionately large number of corporations are formed in Delaware. Most large public companies are incorporated there. Delaware has encouraged corporate formations by adopting laws that favor incumbent officers and directors against attack from dissident shareholders, has a long history of decided court cases interpreting its corporate law, and has no state income tax. These are attractive features to consider when choosing a state for incorporating. Nevada is another state without corporate income tax, and its laws are also designed to actively encourage new corporations.

Limiting Personal Liability

The primary distinguishing feature of a corporation is the so called *limited liability* of the officers, directors, and shareholders (the "principals") of the company. In a properly organized, maintained, and capitalized corporation, the principals have no personal liability for debts of the corporation. If a corporation breaches an obligation or causes injury to a third party, only the corporation and not the principals are legally responsible. If the corporation does not have sufficient assets to satisfy the liability, the creditor is not entitled to seek satisfaction from the personal assets of the principals. This feature is distinct from other businesses operated as sole proprietorships, partnerships, or trusts. In those cases, the owner, partner, or trustee, respectively, has *unlimited liability* for debts incurred in the business.

Effect of Personal Guarantees

Anyone doing business with a corporation may require that the principal of the company give a personal guarantee of a corporate obligation. In simple terms, the person signing a guarantee promises to pay the corporation's debts if the corporation is unable to do so. For example, if you wish to lease office or retail space for the business, the landlord may request a personal guarantee of the lease obligation. If the corporation fails to make its payments on time, the landlord can then collect directly from you. In this manner, a personal guarantee eliminates the benefits of the corporation's limited liability.

Similarly, vendors sometimes will not sell, and banks and other lenders often will not lend to a family corporation without a personal guarantee. To the extent that guarantees are provided, an individual owner will have personal liability for these contracts, and the corporation will not provide protection from these obligations.

Protection from Tort Claims

When the source of the lawsuit is a negligence claim or a claim arising out of the employer-employee relationship, the corporation can be an effective device. We have previously discussed how an employee's negligence may be imputed to his employer. If your secretary injures someone while she is picking up your lunch, you are likely to be responsible for the damages. However, if the secretary is an employee of a corporation, the corporation, but not the officers or directors, will be liable for the injury. This is also the case generally for employee claims of discrimination or wrongful termination. Any such lawsuits will be filed against the corporation as the employer. The principals of the company will not usually be held personally liable for these type of activities.

Protection from Customers

When the corporation *sells* goods or services, liability for these activities will usually be limited to the corporation. A buyer of goods (as opposed to a seller) typically does not require a personal guarantee as to the quality of the product. If the product is faulty or someone is injured by the product, the corporation will be liable but not the principals. If a corporation supplies services, such as contracting or repair work on a house, only the corporation would be liable for faulty services. A corporation provides a useful shield against personal liability in connection with the sale of products or services. When a corporation *buys* goods or services, liability for payment will also be limited to the corporation, unless the principals have signed a personal guarantee of the obligation.

Eliminating Double Taxation

The way corporations are taxed provides some interesting and challenging planning decisions. A corporation is a taxpaying entity. That is, it must file an annual tax return and pay taxes on its income. If those earnings are distributed to a shareholder, this distribution is treated as a *dividend* which is then taxable to the shareholder. The effect of this is that corporate earnings are taxed twice—once at the corporate level and once at the shareholder level, when the earnings are distributed in the form of dividends.

The problem of double taxation may be eliminated in one of two ways. First, the corporation can pay out as salary an amount equal to its net earnings. This is called *zeroing out* the corporation. As an example, a family-owned corporation in the construction business might have a profit of $100,000. If this amount is paid to one or more of the officers of the corporation as compensation for services, the corporation will get a tax deduction for this $100,000 in salary. That will reduce taxable income to zero, and no federal income taxes would be due. The $100,000 is included in income, and the tax is paid by the recipient. This eliminates the problem of double taxation.

The Internal Revenue Code imposes certain limitations on this technique by allowing a deduction to the corporation, only if the amount of compensation paid to a particular individual is "reasonable." The salary cannot be excessive based upon the actual services provided by the individual. There have been thousands of cases litigated by the Internal Revenue Service on this issue, and no firm rule has developed. Basically, if the salary is comparable to that received by others in similar businesses, it is unlikely that there will be a challenge from the IRS.

If you attempt to pay salary to your children or your grandmother without any services performed by them, the deduction could be disallowed as unreasonable. If the salary is disallowed as unreasonable, this amount is added back to the corporation's income and a tax is assessed on this income. Also, the amount which was distributed is treated as a dividend to the recipient and is taxable to that individual. This produces a double tax on the same income and is clearly a disastrous result.

Using S Corporations

The second method for eliminating double taxation is the use of a device called an *S Corporation*. This is a type of corporation specifically provided for in the Internal Revenue Code. An S Corporation is treated differently for tax purposes than a conventional corporation (which is known as a "C Corporation"). If elected by the shareholders, an S Corporation will not be subject to tax at the corporate level. Instead, all corporate income is included directly in the income of the shareholders. There is no need to zero out the corporation with salaries since corporate income is now subject to tax only once, at the shareholder level. Additionally, if the corporation has a *net loss*, that loss can be used by the shareholders to offset other business income.

In order to qualify, the stock of an S Corporation must be held by thirty-five or fewer individuals and all shareholders must consent to the election. An S Corporation has all of the lawsuit protection features of a C Corporation. If unreasonable compensation is an issue or the corporation is expected to show net losses, an S Corporation would be a useful planning technique.

Piercing
The Corporate Veil

The lawsuit protection features of the corporation will be available only if the integrity of the corporation as a separate and distinct entity, apart from the individual, is respected by a court and by the Internal Revenue Service. In matters involving a lawsuit by an injured party, especially if a corporation has no significant assets, the plaintiff will attempt to convince the court that the corporate entity should not be respected and that the principals of the company should be personally liable. In these cases, the plaintiff is attempting to *pierce the corporate veil* in order to obtain a judgment against the principals, who may have personal assets sufficient to satisfy a judgment.

There are many reported cases on this topic, and the outcome is usually determined by whether the corporation carries out its business and looks and acts the way a corporation should. If the principals treat the corporation and hold out the corporation to third parties as a separate and distinct entity, the court will usually uphold the status of the corporation and will not find personal liability. However, if various corporate formalities are not consistently observed, the corporation will be disregarded and the individuals may be held personally liable.

One of the major problems with the corporate format for small businesses is that as a matter of course the shareholders, officers, and directors will be named in any lawsuit against the corporation. The plaintiff will attempt to pierce the corporation or will argue some theory to make the defendants responsible. In a significant number of these cases, when there is a judgment against the corporation, the court will disregard the legal protection of the corporation and will hold the defendant shareholders, officers, or directors liable.

Much of the practical protection offered by the corporate form is rendered meaningless by these cases. Sometimes the protection is upheld, and sometimes it is not. This lack of certainty makes business planning—and sleeping at night—difficult. Since the shareholder will almost always be named as a defendant in the lawsuit, even if he is ultimately successful, the attorney's fees and the costs of defense can be financially ruinous.

There are two solutions to this problem. If you are a principal shareholder or officer/director of a corporation, use a proper asset protection plan to shield your personal assets from the potential liability associated with the corporation. Alternatively, use a Limited Liability Company (LLC)—instead of a corporation to conduct business. We will discuss the LLC in detail, but for now, you should know that an LLC cannot be pierced like a corporation and the members cannot be named in a lawsuit for failure to follow any formalities. It provides the protection against liability associated with the corporation but avoids many of the pitfalls. When considering the best asset protection strategy for your situation, determine whether the LLC is an appropriate form to conduct your business activity.

If you are using a corporation, you must pay attention to formalities which the courts have determined to be of particular significance:

Corporate Bylaws. The corporation must adopt a set of bylaws, which provide a written statement of how the internal affairs of the corporation will be handled. The bylaws set the time and place of regular shareholder meetings and meetings of the board of directors.

Corporate Minute Book. The corporate minute book contains a written record of actions by the shareholders and directors of the corporation. At a minimum, there must be annual minutes reflecting the election of directors by the shareholders. Any significant corporate activities, including corporate borrowings, purchases, and the payment of compensation to officers, should be properly reflected in the minutes of the meetings of the directors and shareholders.

Stock Ledger Book. The corporation must maintain an accurate stock ledger book. This book shows who has been issued stock certificates and the amounts received by the corporation for the issuance of its stock. The stock ledger book contains an up-to-date record of the names and number of shares owned by each shareholder.

Conducting Business in Corporate Name. When doing business with third parties, the officers and directors must make it clear that they are acting on behalf of the corporation and not in their individual capacity. Correspondence should be sent out under the proper corporate letterhead, and contracts should be entered into only with the corporation as a signatory. Unless the documents clearly reflect that a transaction is entered into on behalf of the corporation and all necessary agreements are entered into under the corporation's name, the corporate entity will not survive a challenge in a lawsuit.

Bank Accounts. Corporate bank accounts and accounting records must be separate and distinct from the individual. A corporate bank account cannot be treated as if it were the account of an individual officer or director. Corporate income and assets must be separately accounted for on the books of the corporation. One of the biggest mistakes made by clients is that they feel free to move money and property back and forth between themselves and their corporation without properly accounting for such movement in the records of the corporation. This is a fatal mistake, and under these circumstances, the corporate entity will be disregarded by the court.

Protecting
Corporate Assets

We must also consider the issue of protecting the assets of the corporation. The corporation, as an entity operating a business, is in the front line of attack for litigation from every conceivable source. If the company loses a lawsuit, all of its assets are available for collection. Because of this, a sensible asset protection strategy must be adopted for the corporation as well as for the individual. As a rule, to the extent practical, you do not want the corporation to hold any significant assets. You do not want a corporation to build up a substantial net worth only to see everything wiped out in the event of a lawsuit.

Real Estate and Equipment

Assets, such as real estate and equipment, should never be held by the corporation. These assets should be held by another entity— a Family Limited Partnership, LLC, or a trust—and leased back to the corporation at a reasonable rent. Since the property will be leased, rather than owned, the assets will not be available for collection by a creditor of the corporation.

Surplus Cash

The corporation should never hold any surplus cash. You would be amazed at how often clients proudly tell us that they have accumulated $1 million of cash in a Merrill-Lynch CMA account. This is pure madness. Only amounts necessary to pay immediate and foreseeable obligations should remain in the corporate account. Any surplus should be loaned or paid out as salary or some other type of distribution. The last thing you want is a fat pile of cash sitting around waiting for a creditor.

Inventory and Accounts Receivable

Certain types of property can't be conveniently held outside of the corporation. Assets, such as inventory and accounts receivable, will undoubtedly cause tax and accounting difficulties, unless they are maintained in corporate form.

If these types of assets are significant in value, one solution is to create liens which will have priority over subsequent creditors. For example, the owners of the business can make loans to the corporation for working capital or other needs. As security for these advances, the corporation can give the owners, as collateral, a lien on corporate inventory and receivables. This security interest is called a UCC-1 filing under the provisions of the Uniform Commercial Code (UCC). The hoped for result of this UCC-1 filing is that the inventory and receivables will be protected. A judgment creditor would find that the equity in these assets is subject to the superior claim of the business owners and cannot be used to satisfy the judgment.

Multiple Corporations

If the business of the corporation can be divided into separate businesses, assets can be protected through the use of multiple corporations. For example, a single corporation may own and operate six retail stores in different locations. If something happens at one of the stores, giving rise to potential liability, the assets of the other successful stores must be isolated from these claims.

A client of ours had four fast food restaurants in different locations. All of the stores were held in one corporation. Business at one of the locations slowed down substantially. That store became a financial drain on the others, absorbing all of the available cash in the company. Eventually, the corporation had to file for bankruptcy, wiping out all of the equity that had been built up.

Our approach would have been to have each restaurant separately incorporated. Then, if one business were to falter, it would not drag down the others. A judgment creditor of one corporation would not be able to reach the assets of the other companies. An extreme illustration of this is the taxicab company which separately incorporated twenty-six different taxis.

This strategy is also useful for a company that manufactures or wholesales different product lines. Companies in the pharmaceutical business face enormous potential liability for many types of drugs and medical devices. Several years ago A. H. Robbins was forced into bankruptcy by liability in connection with the IUDs it produced. Dow Corning had similar problems from the liability associated with the silicone breast implants. Whenever a particular product may be hazardous, using multiple corporations is an effective technique for insulating each separate product from liability caused by another.

Protecting Trademarks and Trade Names

Trademarks, patents, and copyrights are valuable assets which should not be owned directly by the operating entity. A separate company can own these assets and make them available through a form of a licensing agreement. The objective is to protect these assets in the event of a judgment against the corporation.

One of our clients was in the garment manufacturing business. His company sold primarily to the large department stores. This is always a dangerous business. A large amount of capital is needed to fill orders which are not paid until sixty or ninety days after shipment. A common scenario goes like this: An unusually large order is placed by a retailer, and the manufacturer uses all of its cash and credit to buy the materials and pay the workers to fill and ship the order. Then, ninety days later, before the manufacturer has gotten paid, the truck pulls up with the entire order returned. Since the value of the goods to the manufacturer is only a fraction of the invoice amount, the manufacturer is now out of business since it is out of cash and out of credit. The bankruptcy court and the creditors now attempt to seize and sell every asset of the company including any valuable trademark or trade name.

Our client engaged in the proper planning before these events took place. The trademark and the trade name were owned by a separate company. The new company (NewCo) then licensed the use of these properties to the corporation on a monthly basis. When the corporation ultimately filed for bankruptcy (because of the circumstances we just described), the trademark and trade name were safely protected in NewCo. Since it was these assets which contained all of the goodwill of the business, our client was able to successfully go back into business and establish a new company.

Using Corporations to Protect Personal Assets

Is a corporation a good strategy for shielding personal assets from potential lawsuits? This is a question which has produced needless confusion and misleading advice. There are many heavily promoted schemes—generally involving Nevada corporations—which claim to provide a myriad of asset protection benefits.

Our view is that the corporation is generally a poor choice as a vehicle to protect assets. It is clumsy, inefficient, and usually better methods will be available.

The source of the problem is that a judgment creditor can seize any shares of stock which you own. If you transfer assets to a corporation in exchange for stock, the creditor simply takes the stock certificates and becomes the owner of those shares. If he obtains more than 50 percent of the shares, the creditor is then in control of the company—and your assets. We will see that this result differs from the Family Limited Partnership or LLC arrangement where the creditor cannot get the right to vote or manage the entity and, therefore, cannot reach the assets held by the company. Since the shares of stock of a corporation are reachable by judgment creditors, a corporation will not provide a significant degree of asset protection, in the event of a successful lawsuit against you.

Some degree of asset protection can be accomplished if you move the shares into a protected position. For example, corporate shares can sometimes be transferred to an entity that provides necessary legal protection for assets such as a Family Limited Partnership (FLP), LLC, or a Privacy Trust. But there are lots of rules and tax traps for the unwary. For instance, shares in an S Corporation cannot be held by an FLP or LLC. Also, only certain types of trusts are permitted shareholders. Hazardous and unintended tax consequences occur frequently with corporations, and so all transactions should be carefully planned and monitored.

Using Corporations for Financial Privacy

Conducting business in a corporation can sometimes create financial privacy advantages. The corporation is a separate entity for legal purposes. It is required to obtain a Federal Tax Identification number, which is separate from the Social Security number of the owner. Real estate, bank accounts, and other business interests can be legally owned in the name of a corporation.

The identity of the shareholders of a corporation is not required in any public filing with the state regarding the incorporation or maintenance of the company. In theory, at least, the names of the shareholders are private and evidence of your ownership is not available for public access. But there are many holes in this general principle. Companies with publicly traded shares are required to disclose the names of principal shareholders in regular reports to the Securities and Exchange Commission and various state regulatory agencies.

The identity of the shareholders of privately held companies must be maintained in a written record in the stock ledger book of the company which is as secure as the procedures implemented by the custodian of the corporate records. In addition, information about the stockholders of a private company may be developed by the database services through voluntary disclosure on credit and insurance applications, business and professional licenses, and other regulatory filings. Those who wish to maintain privacy for the ownership of corporate stock—publicly or privately held—generally use a form of the Privacy Trust which we will discuss in chapter 9.

All corporations must annually file, with the state, the names and addresses of corporate officers and directors. If you are listed as an officer or director, a database search will reveal this connection to your corporation. It doesn't matter which state you have chosen to incorporate in—Nevada, California, Delaware—every state has the same requirement and the information is publicly available.

Let's say that, in order to maximize your privacy, you have a friend or business associate serve as the sole officer and director of the corporation. Alternatively, there are companies and individuals who offer these services, for a fee, to newly formed or existing corporations, mostly in Nevada. They promise to follow directions and act as your agent with regard to the corporation. For convenience, we will call your "friend" Gumby. Gumby's name—but not yours—will now be recorded publicly. If he carefully executes all corporate filings and documents, your name will probably not show up in a search of the databases.

The more difficult privacy issue involves the matter of signature authority with regard to corporate assets. Who should be authorized to sign on the corporate bank account? Although the account itself is in the name of the corporation—with its own Federal Tax Identification number the law requires that the bank obtain the name and Social Security number of *every account signatory*. If you are a signatory on the account you must supply this information. Your name and Social Security number on the account then provides the link to you—exactly what you were trying to avoid in the first place.

You can eliminate this difficulty by having Gumby as the account signatory—but you have now created serious dangers for yourself. You have made Gumby the sole officer, director, and signatory for all corporate assets—presumably valuable to you or you wouldn't be going to this much trouble. In essence, you have turned over to Gumby much of what you own. As attorneys, we see so many risks and opportunities for fraud with this type of arrangement that we don't recommend it for our clients.

One of the largest companies supplying these services was recently raided as part of an IRS crackdown. Computers and files were seized, and criminal investigations are proceeding. Imagine the inconvenience of getting Gumby's signature on a check when he is operating from the federal penitentiary. If your goal is financial privacy, we will show you that there are safer and more efficient alternatives which will accomplish the desired result.

Summary

We have seen that the corporation can provide benefits by limiting the liability of business owners from particular sources of lawsuits. A corporation will be especially effective in situations involving negligence claims and disputes with customers. However, lawsuit protection will be lost if the corporate entity is disregarded by the courts, a very real risk for most smaller companies. In attempting to preserve the sanctity of the corporation as a separate and distinct entity, proper minutes and accounting records must be maintained. Correspondence and contracts with third parties also must clearly establish that it is the corporation, and not the individual, which is conducting the business.

Because of the risk of being named as a defendant in a lawsuit against the corporation, the principal owners, officers, and directors should carefully protect their personal assets from this potential liability. Corporate assets can and should be protected through multiple entities and a variety of asset protection strategies to make the company an unattractive lawsuit target. If permissible, corporate shares must then be held by an entity such as the Family Limited Partnership, Limited Liability Company, or Privacy Trust in order to prevent a creditor from seizing the stock.

The corporate format poses a variety of issues regarding financial privacy. Although there are no public records of the shareholders of privately held companies, considerable information is available from insurance and credit applications and government regulatory compliance. Signature authority over corporate assets will also provide an easily discernible trail leading to your door. Gumby's services can be used to act as agent for signing on accounts and corporate documents, but they are notoriously unreliable and present significant dangers from fraud or other malfeasance. In chapter 9, we will see how Privacy Trusts have been used to solve many of these problems and to accomplish privacy objectives.

CHAPTER SIX

When to Use a Family Limited Partnership

O VER THE PAST FIVE YEARS, the Family Limited Partnership (FLP) has risen from obscurity, as a little known tax loophole, into the preeminent vehicle for asset protection and estate planning. A recent article in *Forbes* extolling the benefits of the FLP—headlined "Cut Your Estate Taxes in Half"—claimed that individuals were successfully using this technique to discount the value of their estate by up to 90 percent.

In this chapter, we will discuss the features of the Family Limited Partnership which provide remarkable advantages and planning opportunities. Although it is not the preferred technique for financial privacy, by itself, or in combination with other techniques, the FLP can be used to create a powerful strategy for asset protection and for realizing estate tax and income tax benefits. We will start with the background on this technique.

Different Types of Partnerships

General Partnerships

A partnership is formed when two or more persons agree to carry on a business together. This agreement can be written or oral. A *general partnership* is formed when two or more people intend to work together to carry on a business activity. No local or state filings are required to create this type of partnership. This is different than a corporation, which does not come into existence until Articles of Incorporation have been filed with the Secretary of State.

The distinguishing feature of a partnership is the *unlimited liability* of the partners. Each partner is personally liable for all of the debts of the partnership. That includes any debts incurred by any of the other partners on behalf of the partnership. Any one partner is able to bind the partnership by entering into a contract on behalf of the partnership. If Jackson and Wilson are partners, and Wilson signs a contract on behalf of the partnership, Jackson will be personally liable for the full amount. This is true regardless of whether Jackson authorized the contract or whether he even knew of its existence. This feature of unlimited liability contrasts with the limited liability of the owners of a corporation. As discussed previously, when a contract is entered into on behalf of a corporation, the owners are not personally liable for its performance.

Because each of the partners has unlimited personal liability, a general partnership is the single most dangerous form for conducting one's business. Not only is a partner liable for contracts entered into by other partners, each partner is also liable for the other partner's negligence. When two or more physicians or other professionals practice together as a partnership, each partner is liable for the negligence or malpractice of any other partner.

In addition, each partner is personally liable for the *entire* amount of any partnership obligation. For example, Doctor Smith may be one of ten partners in a medical partnership, but he is not responsible for only 10 percent of partnership obligations. He is responsible for 100 percent—even though he owns only a 10 percent interest. If Doctor Smith's other partners are unable to pay their respective shares, he must pay the entire amount.

Limited Partnerships

Obviously, the unlimited liability feature of general partnerships is a serious impediment to conducting business using a partnership format. To mitigate the harsh impact of these rules, every state has enacted legislation allowing the formation of a type of partnership known as a *limited partnership*.

A limited partnership consists of one or more *general partners* and one or more *limited partners*. The same person can be both a general partner and a limited partner, as long as there are at least two legal persons who are partners in the partnership. The general partner is responsible for the management of the affairs of the partnership, and he has unlimited personal liability for all debts and obligations.

Limited partners have no personal liability. The limited partner stands to lose only the amount which he has contributed and any amounts which he has obligated himself to contribute under the terms of the partnership agreement. Limited partnerships are often used as investment vehicles for large projects requiring a considerable amount of cash. Individual limited partners contributing

AN EXAMPLE OF A LIMITED PARTNERSHIP

Able and Baker form a limited partnership with Able as the general partner and Baker as the limited partner. Baker contributes $100,000. Able will run the day-to-day affairs of the business, and Baker will provide all of the initial capital. If Able enters into a contract that causes the partnership to incur a liability of $500,000, Baker will lose his $100,000 contribution, but he has no obligation to contribute any additional funds. Able, as the general partner, has personal liability for the entire amount. He has no right to demand that Baker make any further contributions.

money to a venture, but not having management powers, will not have any personal liability for the debts of the business.

In exchange for this protection against personal liability, a limited partner may not actively participate in management. However, it is permissible for a limited partner to have a vote on certain matters, just as a shareholder has a right to vote on some corporate matters. A typical limited partnership agreement may provide that a majority vote of the limited partners is necessary for the sale of assets or to remove a general partner. The partnership agreement determines whether the limited partners can vote on these matters.

If a limited partner assumes an active role in management, that partner may lose his limited liability protection and may be treated as a general partner. For instance, if a limited partner negotiates a contract with a third party on behalf of the partnership, the limited partner may have liability as a general partner. For this reason, a limited partner's activities must be carefully circumscribed.

Tax Treatment of Partnerships

Since the partnership is a "pass through" entity, there is no potential for income tax on it. Unlike corporations and irrevocable trusts, a partnership is not a taxpaying entity. A partnership files an annual informational tax return setting forth its income and expenses, but it doesn't pay tax on its net income. Instead, each partner's proportionate share of income or loss is passed through from the partnership to the individual. Each partner claims his share of deductions or reports his share of income on his own tax return.

This avoids the potential for double taxation that is always present in a C Corporation. Typically, when a business is expected to show a net loss rather than a gain, the partnership format is used so that the losses can be used by the partners. Limited partnerships have always been used for real estate and tax shelter investments in order to pass the tax deductions through to the individual investors. These losses are then used by the partner to offset other income he might have. Although the Tax Reform Act of 1986 now limits the ability to immediately deduct losses from "passive activities" to offset wages or investment income, the partnership format may still be desirable if the circumstances of the individual partner are such that he is able to take advantage of these losses.

The rules regarding the taxation of partnership activities are lengthy and cumbersome. As a general rule, however, transfers of property into and out of a partnership will not ordinarily produce any tax consequences.

Lawsuit Protection

The Family Limited Partnership is an outstanding device for providing lawsuit protection for family wealth. When used as part of a properly designed overall strategy, usually with the Privacy Trust, an unsurpassed level of asset protection can be accomplished.

Under the typical arrangement, the FLP is set up so that Husband and Wife are each general partners. As such, they may own only a 1 or 2 percent interest in the partnership. The remaining interests are in the form of limited partnership interests. These interests will be held, directly or indirectly, by Husband, Wife, or other family members, depending upon a variety of factors which will be discussed.

After setting up the FLP, all family assets are transferred into it, including investments and business interests. When the transfers are complete, Husband and Wife no longer own a direct interest in these assets. Instead, they own a controlling interest in the FLP, and it is the FLP which owns the assets. As general partners, they have complete management and control over the affairs of the partnership and can buy or sell any assets they wish. They have the right to retain in the partnership proceeds from the sale of any partnership assets, or they can distribute these proceeds out to the partners.

Creditor Cannot Reach Assets

Now, let's see what happens if there is a lawsuit against either Husband or Wife. Assume that Husband is a physician and that there is a malpractice judgment against him for $1 million. The plaintiff in the action is now a judgment creditor, and he will try to collect the $1 million from Husband.

The judgment creditor would like to seize Husband's bank accounts and investments in order to collect the amount which he is owed. However, he discovers that Husband no longer holds title to any of these assets. In fact, since all of these assets have been transferred to the FLP, the only asset held by Husband is his interest in the FLP. Can the creditor reach into the partnership and seize the investments and bank accounts?

The answer is no. Under the provisions of the Uniform Limited Partnership Act, *a creditor of a partner cannot reach into the partnership and take specific partnership assets*. The creditor has no rights to any property which is held by the partnership. Since title to the assets is in the name of the partnership and it is the Husband partner rather than the partnership which is liable for the debt, partnership assets may not be taken to satisfy the judgment.

Charging Order Remedy

If a judgment creditor cannot reach partnership assets, what can he do? Since Husband's only asset is an interest in the FLP, the creditor would apply to the court for a *charging order* against Husband's partnership interest. A charging order means that the general partner is directed to pay over to the judgment creditor any distributions from the partnership which would otherwise go the debtor partner, until the judgment is paid in full. In other words, money which comes out of the partnership to the debtor partner can be seized by the creditor until the amount of the judgment is satisfied. Cash distributions paid to Husband could, therefore, be taken by the creditor. A charging order does *not* give the creditor the right to become a partner in the partnership and does *not* give him any right to interfere in the management or control of partnership affairs. He only receives the right to any actual distributions paid to Husband.

Under the circumstances in which a creditor has obtained a charging order, the partnership would not make any distributions to the debtor partner. This arrangement would be provided for in the partnership agreement and is permissible under partnership law. If the partnership does not make any distributions, the judgment creditor will not receive any payments. The partnership simply retains all of its funds and continues to invest and reinvest its cash without making any distributions.

The result of this technique is that family assets have been successfully protected from the judgment against Husband. Had the FLP arrangement not been used and had Husband and Wife kept all of their assets in their own names, the judgment creditor would have seized everything. Instead, through the use of this technique, all of these assets were protected.

Reason for This Law

The law prohibiting a creditor from reaching the assets of the partnership has been well established for many years. In fact, these particular provisions of partnership law were first adopted as part of the English Partnership Act of 1890 and were subsequently adopted as part of the Uniform Partnership Act, which has been the basis of the law in the United States since the 1940s.

The reason for these provisions is that they are necessary to accomplish a particular public policy objective. This policy is that the business activities of a partnership should not be disrupted because of non-partnership related debts of one of the partners. Prior to the adoption of these provisions, it was possible for a creditor of a partner to obtain a Writ of Execution ordering the local sheriff to levy directly on the property of the partnership to satisfy the creditor's debt. The local sheriff went to the partnership's place of business, shut down the business, seized all of the assets, and sold them to satisfy the debt. These methods not only destroyed the partnership's business but also caused a significant economic injustice to the non-debtor partner through the forced liquidation of partnership assets. The non-debtor partner didn't do anything wrong. Why should he be forced to suffer?

To avoid precisely these unfair results, the law was formulated so that a creditor with a judgment against a partner—but not against the partnership—cannot execute directly on partnership assets. Instead, the law allows the creditor to obtain a charging order, which affects only the actual distributions made to the debtor partner. The business of the partnership is allowed to continue unhampered, and the economic interest of the non-debtor partner is not impaired.

The protection of partnership assets from the claims of one partner's creditors is deeply entrenched in the foundation of American and English partnership law. Without such protection, the formation of partnerships would be discouraged and legitimate business activities would be impeded. When understood in this light, it is clear that the asset protection features of a Family Limited Partnership are neither a fluke nor a loophole in the law. Rather, these provisions are an integral part of partnership design, and it is unlikely that changes in the law will ever be made which would impair these features.

How to Save Income and Estate Taxes

Income Tax Benefits

If family assets are held in the form of a limited partnership, it will be possible to obtain certain income tax savings in addition to the asset protection benefits. Tax savings can be realized by spreading income from high tax bracket parents to lower tax bracket children and grandchildren who are fourteen years or older. Let's look at an example of how this might work:

One of our clients had taxable income from various investments of approximately $200,000, consisting of interest and dividends from bonds, stocks, and trust deeds that he owned. He was in a 32 percent maximum tax bracket and paid taxes of approximately $64,000 per year on this income. As part of an overall business plan that we established, all of his assets were transferred into a Family Limited Partnership and a total of seven children and grand-children were brought in as limited partners of the partnership. Under the partnership agreement, the children and grandchildren were taxable on $100,000 of the $200,000 in income generated by the partnership. Each of these children was in a maximum tax bracket of 15 percent, and thus, the total taxes owed on this $100,000 of investment income was reduced from $32,000 to $15,000. This produced a savings of $17,000 in overall family in-come taxes. Under the partnership agreement it was not required that the $100,000 actually be distributed to the children. In fact, the parents as general partners retained all of this amount except for what was needed to pay the taxes on the children's share of partnership income. The parents thereby reduced their annual in-come taxes by shifting a substantial amount of income to their children. The tax savings were held as a college fund for the grand-children.

Estate Tax Benefits

We can also use the Family Limited Partnership as a vehicle for dramatically reducing or eliminating estate taxes. This estate tax reduction can be accomplished because of certain unique attributes of the FLP which are not present in any other business entity. Of primary importance is the ability to shift the value of assets out of your estate without any concomitant loss of control, through a program of gifting limited partnership interests to your children or other family members.

For example, the Smith family owns a business with a current value of $1 million, a rental property with equity of $500,000, and retirement savings in stocks and bonds equal to $1 million. That's a total estate of $2.5 million. Under current law, with a properly designed estate plan, taking maximum advantage of the combined current exemption of $1.3 million, the estate tax on the balance of $1.2 million would be approximately $500,000. Mr. and Mrs. Smith would like to take steps to preserve the family estate for the benefit of their three children, but they do not wish to give up control over their assets during their lifetime.

One solution to the problem involves a properly structured estate plan including an FLP that is established to hold all family assets. Mr. and Mrs. Smith would be the general partners of the FLP. As such they would have complete management and control over their property in the FLP. Initially, they could make a gift of the limited partnership interests to their children in an amount equal in value to the combined maximum estate tax credit (currently $1.3 million). In subsequent years, they could gift limited partnership interests equal to the amount of the annual gift tax exclusion of $20,000 per child ($60,000 per year).

Under this approach, in roughly seventeen years, the Smiths would be able to eliminate potential estate taxes and could preserve $500,000 of family wealth. At the same time that the Smiths are accomplishing this result, they would not relinquish any degree of control or authority over their real estate or their retirement savings.

That's not a bad result, but we can push the advantages a great deal further. According to IRS rulings and court cases, the value of each gift of a limited partnership interest must be *discounted* in order to account for the lack of marketability and the lack of control associated with those interests. For example, if the parents transfer assets with a value of $1 million to an FLP, a gift of a 1 percent limited partnership interest should not be valued at $10,000. Instead, because the interest cannot be readily sold and because the donee has no right to participate in management of the FLP, a reasonable approach to determine value, suggested by many financial advisors, would be to discount the transferred interest to reflect its true value in the market. Discounts in the range of 30 percent are fairly conservative, but some aggressive advisors push this number to the 50 percent range.

Once this discount is taken into consideration, potential tax savings can be accelerated. Using an aggressive 40 percent discount, the value of the limited partnership interests in the Smith FLP would be discounted in value from $2.5 million to $1.5 million. Almost all of this value could be gifted in the first year without exceeding the credit of $1.3 million. The remaining $200,000 in value could be transferred out of their estate in just one or two years. In a relatively painless fashion, the Smiths have eliminated $500,000 of estate taxes while maintaining control over their assets. If a less aggressive discount is chosen, it might take five or six years to completely eliminate the tax instead of one or two years as we just illustrated.

As an added bonus, this approach will also remove future appreciation from the Smiths' estate. In our example, the rental property and the business have a value today of $1.5 million. Increasing in value at a rate of just 7 percent per year, these assets would be worth an *additional* $1.5 million in just ten years. That's another $750,000 in estate taxes that the Smiths have avoided by the use of the FLP strategy. If you own real estate or a business which you believe will increase in value over the years, the FLP provides an excellent planning opportunity to achieve meaningful estate tax savings.

You should note that the FLP, like all tax planning strategies, is likely to be attacked by the IRS if the requisite formalities are not properly followed. Although Congress has rejected attempts by the Administration to eliminate these benefits and the IRS has not been successful in challenging the FLP in court, those who claim highly aggressive discounts or establish the FLP in near death circumstances can anticipate some level of opposition. As a general rule, if you are using the FLP to achieve estate tax savings, make sure that:

1. A credible appraisal is obtained to support the amount of the discount which is claimed.

2. The documents are properly drafted.

3. There is a sound purpose for the plan other than tax avoidance (such as asset protection or privacy).

Creating the Family Limited Partnership

The first step in creating the Family Limited Partnership is the preparation and filing of the Certificate of Limited Partnership with the Secretary of State. The form asks for the name of the limited partnership. This name should be cleared in advance with the Secretary of State's office because the filing will not be accepted if the name is similar to another name already on file. The Certificate of Limited Partnership also asks for the name of a designated Agent for the Service of Process, which is the name and address of a person (or company) who is authorized by the partnership to receive service of process if the partnership is sued for any reason. Any family member residing in the state can be designated as the agent. There are also companies that will, for a modest fee, act as the designated agent for these purposes.

The form also asks for the names and addresses of all general partners of the partnership. The names of the limited partners are not required. Since this document is a matter of public record, the names of the general partners will be publicly available but not the names of the limited partners. Along with the Certificate of

Limited Partnership, each state requires a filing fee which is usually about $85–$125.

When the Secretary of State's office receives the properly filled out form, with an acceptable partnership name, the Certificate will be filed. At this point, the partnership will be legally formed. You should request that a certified copy of the Certificate of Limited Partnership be returned to you, and your copy should be stamped with the filing date. It is essential that you have at least one certified copy for opening a bank or brokerage account, or for the purchase or sale of real estate in the name of the partnership.

The Partnership Agreement

Concurrently with the filing of the Certificate of Limited Partnership, a written partnership agreement must be prepared. This is the document that governs the affairs of the partnership. It sets out the purpose of the partnership, the duties of the general partners, matters on which the vote of the limited partners is required, the share of partnership capital and profits to which each partner is entitled, and all other matters affecting the relations between the partners.

When creating a Family Limited Partnership for estate planning and asset protection purposes, the partnership agreement must also contain certain key provisions designed to accomplish your objectives. Taken together, these provisions must ensure that a creditor can never achieve any influence over partnership affairs and that Husband and Wife, as general partners, always maintain absolute control over the assets of the partnership. These provisions are unique and essential to a properly structured Family Limited Partnership.

Funding the Partnership

The next step in the partnership formation process is the funding of the partnership. That means you must now decide which assets to transfer and the best means for doing so.

Dangerous and Safe Assets

In making the decision about funding the partnership, it is important that you understand the distinction between Safe Assets and Dangerous Assets.

Safe Assets are those which do not, by themselves, produce a high degree of lawsuit risk. For instance, if you own investment securities such as stocks, bonds, or mutual funds, it is unlikely that these assets will cause you to be sued. Mere ownership of investment assets, without some active involvement in the underlying business, would probably not cause a significant degree of lawsuit exposure.

Dangerous Assets, on the other hand, are those which, by their nature, create a substantial risk of liability. These are generally active business type assets, rental real estate, or motor vehicle ownership, any of which may cause you to be sued.

The reason for the distinction between Safe Assets and Dangerous Assets is that you do not wish to have the FLP incur liability because of its ownership of a Dangerous Asset. If the partnership does incur liability, it will be the target of a lawsuit and all of the assets in that partnership will be subject to the claims of the judgment creditor. This is exactly the situation you are trying to avoid. *Dangerous Assets must either be left outside of the partnership or must be placed in one or more separate entities.* Dangerous Assets must be isolated from each other and from Safe Assets, in order to avoid contaminating the Safe Assets.

Dangerous Assets

An example of a Dangerous Asset is an apartment building. The liability potential of apartment houses is particularly high. Although liability insurance coverage is usually available, the amount of coverage may not be sufficient. A fire in a densely populated building may cause severe injury or death to many tenants. The potential liability for such a tragedy could easily reach into the millions of dollars, exceeding by far the amount of your insurance coverage.

Apartment owners can also be held responsible for the acts of the resident managers. If the resident manager engages in race or sex discrimination in renting to tenants, or is guilty of sexual harassment, this liability may be imputed to you as the owner of the property. Acts such as these may not be covered under your standard insurance coverage.

If this asset is transferred to the same Family Limited Partnership that holds all of your other assets, that partnership, as the owner of the property, will face a high degree of lawsuit exposure and all of your assets will again be at risk.

Instead, the best approach for a Dangerous Asset such as an apartment building is to transfer that property to its own *separate* entity. Generally the Limited Liability Company is the proper way to hold Dangerous Assets. Since no individual member of an LLC can be sued for an LLC related obligation, the liability associated with the Dangerous Asset can be contained and insulated in the LLC. If a number of Dangerous Assets are owned, each should be placed in a separate entity. Once we formed thirty-two different LLCs for a client, each holding one apartment building. If a disaster occurred, only the LLC which owned that property would be sued. The other properties and family assets were safely insulated and shielded from liability under this arrangement.

Some types of commercial real estate may also constitute Dangerous Assets. Office buildings, hotels, restaurants, nightclubs, or any other building where many people work or gather, all have the potential to produce stratospheric liability in the event of some type of disaster. These properties must be kept separate from other types of assets. We will discuss details about the use and operation of the LLC in the next chapter.

Safe Assets

Safe Assets with a low probability of creating lawsuit liability can be maintained in a single Family Limited Partnership.

Although the family home is a Safe Asset, with liability issues generally covered by insurance, there are a number of tax issues which arise with respect to the transfer of the family home into the Family Limited Partnership. The first problem concerns the availability of the income tax deduction for home mortgage interest. Section 163 of the Internal Revenue Code permits a deduction for "qualified residence interest." A "qualified residence" is defined as the "principal residence" of the taxpayer. The only requirements appear to be that (1) the house is the principal residence of the taxpayer; (2) interest is paid by the taxpayer; and (3) the taxpayer has a beneficial interest in any entity that holds legal title to the property. Based upon the language of the statute, the deduction for mortgage interest would, therefore, not seem to be adversely affected by a transfer into the Family Limited Partnership. However, until the law on this issue has been conclusively decided *you should not risk the consequences of a disallowance of your mortgage interest deduction.*

Similar tax issues concern the ability to avoid up to $500,000 of the gain from the sale of your home. It is likely that a transfer of your residence into the FLP would cause you to lose this tax advantage. For these reasons, we do not recommend using the FLP to hold the family residence.

An alternative is to use the Privacy Trust to own the home. All of the tax benefits will be preserved and the highest level of protection can be maintained. We will discuss these issues in the material in chapter 9.

Bank and Brokerage Accounts

These types of accounts do not create any potential liability and can be transferred into the Family Limited Partnership. In order to open these accounts in the name of the partnership, you will present the financial institution with a certified copy of the Certificate of Limited Partnership. The institution will also require the Taxpayer Identification Number issued to the partnership by the Internal Revenue Service.

Interest In Other Entities

The Family Limited Partnership is an excellent vehicle for holding interests in other business entities. The reason that we mention these other business entities is that the Family Limited Partnership must not ever be engaged in any business activities. You do not want the partnership to buy or sell property or goods or to enter into contracts. If the partnership does business, then the partnership can get sued. And if the partnership gets sued and loses, all of the assets that it holds can be lost.

For example, a client of ours entered into a contract to purchase a shopping center. Previously, we had set up a Family Limited Partnership for him. Without our knowledge, the "Buyer" under the purchase contract was the Family Limited Partnership. During the pre-closing escrow period, financing became unavailable and the client failed to complete the deal. The seller sued the partnership for damages for breach of contract and was awarded $600,000 wiping out a substantial portion of our client's assets. The seller sued the partnership because the partnership was the named party to the contract.

This transaction should not have been handled in this manner. The proper way to conduct this type of business activity is through a separate LLC or partnership arrangement. By using the proper planning techniques, potential liability can be significantly reduced and valuable personal assets can be protected from a dangerous lawsuit. Had this arrangement been used, our client would not have lost $600,000. Instead, the buyer and seller would probably have renegotiated the terms of the purchase in a way that was mutually satisfactory to each side.

This example illustrates the necessity for conducting business activities through an entity other than the Family Limited Partnership so that family assets are not exposed to the risk of liability. The proper role of the Family Limited Partnership in this context is to hold the interests in the business entities that are themselves subject to risk. The FLP can hold these interests, providing asset protection and estate planning advantages in a single integrated package.

Financial Privacy With The FLP

In the typical structure, Husband and Wife, or one of them serves as general partner of the FLP. Although the names of the limited partners are not public information, the name of the general partner is required to appear on the Certificate of Limited Partnership filed with the Secretary of State. That creates a privacy problem. Since a search of the limited partnership filings is standard procedure in every financial investigation, your role as general partner will be discovered. A search will then be conducted for real estate or accounts in the name of the FLP, and an accurate picture of FLP assets will be constructed.

This in itself is not necessarily a problem. Assets in the FLP are legally protected from potential claims. Even if assets are discovered, the usefulness of this information is not certain. But for those who want to protect their financial information, the public disclosure of the name of the general partner is an issue that must be resolved.

The second privacy problem that must be overcome—as we discussed in the previous chapter—is the issue of signature authority. Who will sign on the FLP bank account? Clearly, if you are the signatory and your name and Social Security number are listed on the account records, that fact will be discovered by anyone conducting a financial investigation. Privacy is compromised in the FLP and other strategies when you are the signatory for property and accounts in the name of the company.

Both of these privacy obstacles can be successfully resolved with the proper use of a Limited Liability Company and a Privacy Trust. When an LLC owned by the Privacy Trust serves as general partner of the FLP, we can accomplish the desired privacy objectives. This approach and similar strategies will be discussed and illustrated in subsequent chapters as we explore the details of these arrangements.

CHAPTER SEVEN

Powerful Strategies With the Limited Liability Company

THE LIMITED LIABILITY COMPANY (LLC) has become a powerful tool for accomplishing financial privacy and asset protection goals. The LLC is the most versatile and convenient strategy for owning rental property, insulating Dangerous Assets, operating a business, and achieving an excellent level of financial privacy.

Background

The LLC is a relatively new legal entity created by statute and recognized in all fifty states. The adoption of the LLC format began in Wyoming and Florida in the 1970s with approval in most other states only within the last ten years. The purpose of the legislation is to allow individuals to create a legal entity that avoids many of the tax and business problems inherent in the corporate and partnership structure. The intent of the law is to allow individuals to conduct their financial and business affairs in an efficient and convenient manner without the restrictions, formalities, and liabilities associated with those other entities.

More particularly, the LLC provides *the protection from liability* of a corporation without the formalities of corporate minutes, bylaws, directors, and shareholders. In contrast to corporate law, which allows shareholders and officers to be individually sued if the corporate formalities are not followed, the LLC law specifically bars a lawsuit against a member for the liabilities of the LLC. That is an important distinction which you should understand. The principle shareholders and officers of a corporation are routinely named as defendants in a lawsuit against the company—forcing them to incur attorney's fees to defend themselves and rendering the corporate shield meaningless from a practical standpoint.

A primary goal of the LLC legislation was to change this result by clearly stating that the members and managers of the LLC could not be named in a lawsuit against the company. The new law was drawn specifically to provide a vehicle which would protect the owners from liability associated with the business—what the corporation was intended for but no longer accomplished.

The LLC is also convenient to maintain. The owners are permitted to adopt flexible rules regarding the administration and operation of the business. For tax purposes, it is treated like a partnership. That means the LLC itself pays no income tax. All of the income and deductions flow through directly to the members and is reported on their personal tax returns.

The LLC is formed by filing Articles of Organization with the Secretary of State's office. Unlike the FLP which requires the names of the general partners—the disclosure of the names of the principals can be avoided. The name of *either* the member or the manager must be provided in the articles. Also, many states, including

Nevada and Delaware, permit a single member LLC to be formed. We will see that these provisions open the door for a variety of financial privacy strategies. Anonymous ownership of financial accounts, business interests, and real estate can be achieved with an LLC as an important component of the plan.

The LLC Compared to Other Techniques

Inside and Outside Liability

To understand the significant benefits offered by the LLC, let's look at a typical example. John and Mary own an apartment building as tenants-in-common. We know that holding the property, as they do now, exposes them to great danger. Ownership of rental property creates more uncontrolled liability and lawsuit risk than any other business or profession we have seen. And because this potential liability usually cannot be covered by insurance, a single unpredictable event, a mistake, or just bad luck can wipe out everything built up over the years.

Injuries to tenants, problems with lenders, lawsuits from future buyers—all subject everything that John and Mary own to potential liabilities from the property. We call this type of liability, arising from the property itself—*inside liability*. John and Mary need to be protected from *inside liability*.

To make matters worse, a lawsuit or claim against John or Mary from a matter not related to the building exposes the equity in the apartment property to seizure in satisfaction of that claim. We call this type of liability *outside liability*. John and Mary's interest in the property must be protected from outside liability. If one of them is involved in an auto accident causing serious injury, they do not want to lose the property because of this outside liability. Clearly, owning the apartment building in the current manner is not sound business planning. What other options are available to them?

LLC versus Corporation

John and Mary could transfer the property to a corporation. Each would own 50 percent of the stock in the company. Since the law provides that the shareholders are not responsible for debts of the corporation, a liability arising out of the property would not subject John and Mary's personal assets to danger.

The problem is that this protection against liability is only available if all of the corporate formalities are carefully followed. Since most people do not maintain proper corporate records and documentation, corporations often do not provide the intended level of protection. Further, corporations are subject to complex tax rules, which can cause severe and unintended consequences.

Finally, the corporation will not protect the property from outside liability—lawsuits against John or Mary unrelated to the property. A creditor can simply seize the stock that they own and reach the apartment building by dissolving the company. For these reasons, it is generally not advisable to hold investment real estate in a corporation.

LLC versus Limited Partnership

If John and Mary form a limited partnership to hold the property, one or both of them will serve as general partner. Since the general partner has unlimited liability for the debts of the partnership, if a liability arises out of the operation of the building, the general partner's assets will be exposed to that claim. The major problem with the limited partnership format is this unlimited liability of the general partner. From a tax standpoint, the limited partnership does not cause any difficulties and, as previously discussed, a creditor suing John or Mary for an outside liability would be limited to a charging order, which would not affect the property in the partnership.

The Benefits of the LLC

By forming an LLC, John and Mary can accomplish all of their objectives.

Protection from Inside Liability

A member of an LLC is not responsible for claims or judgments against the company. When we are dealing with a rental property or an active business, the potential liability associated with the business is a primary concern. But as we have stated, the law specifically provides that the members of the LLC cannot be sued. In our example, John and Mary transfer their apartment building to an LLC. If a tenant is injured in an accident, John and Mary, as members of the company, would be protected from any claim relating to the property.

No Formalities

An LLC is not required to maintain formal minutes and resolutions. Recordkeeping requirements can be minimized without a threat that the members will be sued individually for a liability of the company. Contrast this treatment with that of a corporation. If the proper formalities are not followed, the corporate protection will be pierced and the owners will have liability for company obligations. The LLC law is specifically intended to remedy this problem by providing that the entity cannot be pierced because of a failure to maintain any of the corporate type documents.

Protection from Outside Liability

Property held in an LLC cannot be seized by a creditor of a member. If there is a judgment or claim against John or Mary, the creditor cannot reach the property held in the LLC. As is the case with the Family Limited Partnership, assets of the LLC are protected from potential claims against a member. The creditor is limited to the ineffective charging order remedy. A creditor with a judgment against a member of the LLC is only permitted to take whatever actual cash distributions are made by the company. The creditor cannot force a distribution or demand any portion of the assets of the company.

Financial Privacy

John and Mary value their personal privacy and wish to protect what they own from public disclosure. They accomplish this by using a Privacy Trust to hold all of their membership interests. The only name disclosed in the Articles of Organization and the annual filings is the name of the trust. Their ownership of the property is secret. Nobody will know they own the property unless they voluntarily disclose the fact.

Case Studies

We will give you some real life illustrations to see how these points fit together.

Mrs. Drake was a seventy-five-year-old widow. She sold a duplex she had owned in California for many years for $200,000 and used the money—her life savings—to move to Arizona and buy a condominium. Her only income was Social Security payments of $1,200 per month which she used to pay her living expenses.

Three years after the sale, the real estate market in California collapsed, and the value of the duplex dropped by half. That shouldn't have mattered to Mrs. Drake since she had sold the property three years earlier. The new buyer was just unlucky when he lost his equity in the property.

But that's not how it works anymore. The buyer sued Mrs. Drake in California claiming that she had failed to disclose defects in the property. None of these allegations were true. The reality was that the buyer had lost money when the market declined and he wanted it back. So he asked the court to rescind the sale contract—meaning that he wanted his $200,000 back plus interest.

The lawsuit placed Mrs. Drake in a terrible position. To defend the case she would have to hire an attorney—and these types of cases are expensive. She was told that legal fees to defend her would run from $25,000–$50,000—money she clearly could not afford. The buyer's attorney, on the other hand, was handling the case on a contingency—so the buyer really had no cost and nothing to lose by pursuing the lawsuit.

Rather than risk losing her home and the rest of her savings and knowing that the litigation costs alone could wipe her out, Mrs. Drake settled the case for $70,000. She borrowed the money against the equity in her condominium, and she now uses most of her Social Security check to make the monthly mortgage payment. Instead of a comfortable retirement—enjoying her life—she lives a spartan existence, barely surviving each month.

What did she do wrong? She sold her property at the top of the market. She should be rewarded for her good business sense. Instead, because she was an easy and a vulnerable target, the buyer and his lawyer managed to extort most of her life savings.

What should she have done? The outcome of the case would likely have been different if she had used an LLC and a Privacy Trust to hold her Arizona condominium. Her ownership of the property would have been well concealed. The lawyer for the buyer would not have discovered her ownership of the property, and without assets, she would not have been an attractive defendant. Additionally, the arrangement works so well from an asset protection standpoint, that even if Mrs. Drake had been sued by the buyer—and if she had lost—her home would have been shielded from the judgment. Privacy for assets plus legal protection is a plan which usually defeats these types of extortion attempts.

The next illustration involves a client, Dan, who owned a valuable shopping center for many years. He had paid about $100,000 for it in 1970, and because of depreciation deductions, it had a zero basis for tax purposes. In 1993, when he came to see us, the property had a value of $1 million. He had two principle objectives: First, he wanted to protect this asset from any claims which might arise from his business or personal activities. Second, he wanted to protect himself from any liability associated with the property. He didn't want to get sued because of some problem with the property and risk losing the other assets he had accumulated. He had no pending or threatened lawsuits or other immediate concerns. He was simply interested in developing a prudent business plan.

We felt that these objectives could be accomplished, and as a part of his overall plan, we put the shopping center into an LLC. His other assets, including his home and savings, were transferred into the Privacy Trust. We did not put the shopping center into the Privacy Trust because it is a Dangerous Asset and should not be mixed with Safe Assets such as a residence and savings accounts.

In 1995, Dan become involved in some serious business problems because of a partner in a restaurant venture. The partner refused to pay his share of the expenses, and Dan was stuck with judgments and bills totaling more than $1 million. The creditor with the judgment attempted to collect from Dan. Because the shopping center was in the LLC, the judgment lien did not apply to that property. Dan was free to sell, refinance, or deal with the property as he decided. His bank accounts and brokerage accounts were safely protected in the Privacy Trust. The judgment had virtually no effect on Dan's accumulated assets, because he had engaged in the proper planning.

Compare the difference in Dan's case that resulted from the strategy he used. If he had not put the shopping center in the LLC, the judgment lien would have attached to the property. The creditor would have foreclosed on the property to collect the debt.

For income tax purposes, a foreclosure is treated like a sale for the amount of the debt. In other words, if the creditor had seized the shopping center, Dan would have been treated as if he had sold the property for $1 million. His tax basis was zero so the taxable gain would have been $1 million. Not only would he have lost the property with all that equity—he would have been stuck with a tax bill to the IRS of about $300,000.

Instead he managed to shield his valuable assets and continue to defer the taxes on the shopping center. This is a dramatic example of the advantages which can be obtained by using the correct legal structure to protect valuable assets.

Insulating
Business Risks

In addition to rental real estate, most businesses can be owned and operated in an LLC. In some states, such as California, some types of businesses—physicians and some other licensed professionals— are not permitted to use an LLC for their practice. But the LLC will usually be the proper form of business for most individuals.

The major criteria in selecting the entity within which to conduct a business is the degree of insulation offered from the liabilities of the business. If you already own a business or are planning to start one, do you want to place everything you own at risk?

Any business venture is a Dangerous Asset. There are leases to sign, bank loans, customers, employees, competitors, and government agencies—all with the potential to blow you sky high. You don't want the liabilities from this business to threaten your other assets. The proper strategy is to contain the liabilities within the shield of the LLC. If something happens inside the company, make sure that it doesn't contaminate your savings and other assets. (See "Small Investments Can Create Large Liabilities.")

The decision making process involves understanding the legal risks which are created in the proposed business and creating the proper legal structure to contain those risks.

The purpose of asset protection planning is to allow you to engage in a business activity while protecting your other assets from the risks associated with the business. The proper plan enables you to pursue attractive investments and business opportunities without jeopardizing everything you own. Do you want to buy real estate or start a business? Understand your level of risk and then protect what you have. That's the sensible approach.

SMALL INVESTMENTS CAN CREATE LARGE LIABILITIES

A physician client invested $50,000 in a new restaurant. The arrangement was that he would put up the money, and the other partner would run the business. The doctor did not realize that he would be fully responsible for all debts of the company—even if he never knew about or signed an agreement. In a general partnership, each partner is liable for all partnership obligations, even those incurred by another partner. And, not surprisingly, his partner signed a five-year lease for the restaurant and bought several hundred thousand dollars of equipment on credit. When the business shut down six months later, our client, as the only partner with any money, was responsible for the remaining lease payments and the equipment, all of which totaled more than $500,000.

This case emphasizes that a relatively small investment can create a large liability. The restaurant investor analyzed the business deal based upon what could happen to his initial investment. He thought that in the worst case he would lose his contribution of $50,000. He certainly didn't want that to happen, but he was prepared to risk a certain sum of money. But the amount of the investment is only a part of the equation. He did not think about the extent of the risk to his personal assets created by the liabilities of the business. The real question should always be: "How much trouble and how much money can this deal cost me?"

By now you know that the restaurant business should have been formed as an LLC rather than a partnership. As a member of the LLC ,the investor would not have had any liability and could not have lost more than his initial contribution.

Other Dangerous Assets

Elderly Drivers

A client asked us to set up a plan for his elderly mother whom we will call Louise. She was eighty-four years old and owned a home and some savings. She was in good health and drove her car to do errands and visit with friends every day. Louise had been in two minor fender benders in the past three years, and our client was concerned that there could be a more serious accident—one in which Louise or an innocent party would be injured.

In this case, Louise's car was the Dangerous Asset, capable of producing a large lawsuit liability if she got into an accident. Since adequate insurance was impossible to obtain, it was necessary to create an asset protection plan which would protect Louise's home and savings if the worst happened. We put her home into a Privacy Trust and her investments into an LLC. Six months later there was indeed an accident, and both passengers in the other car had bruises and broken arms.

The lawyers for the plaintiffs ran an extensive asset search on Louise to see if they should proceed with the case. They found that there were no reachable assets, except her car, and they accepted the insurance company's offer of the $100,000 policy limits. Louise managed to avoid a devastating financial loss, and she held on to her home and savings.

Teenage Drivers

A client in the stock brokerage business set up a plan to protect his savings from potential liability associated with his business. He and his wife went to Mexico for a vacation, leaving his eighteen year old son at home. The son had a party, got drunk, and crashed the family car causing serious injury to three other people.

An automobile is a Dangerous Asset, because anyone is capable of an accident that results in catastrophic injury. It is possible to cause injury that exceeds the amount of any reasonable insurance coverage. In particular, if there are teenage drivers, anyone who might drive while intoxicated, or an elderly driver whose abilities are somehow impaired, it is essential to isolate the auto from the other assets of the family.

Keep Your Property Free From Attachments and Liens

The most powerful weapon of a potential legal adversary is his ability to freeze your assets. When your bank account is frozen, it means nothing can be moved. You cannot pay your bills, run your business, or withdraw your money. Your residence or rental property or business can also be attached. You can't collect rents or income, and your property cannot be sold or refinanced.

The plaintiff can attach your property *during* or *after* the lawsuit. An attachment during the case is known as a pre-judgment attachment; an attachment after the case is decided is called a judgment lien. A pre-judgment attachment is only granted in certain types of cases, generally those involving a contract dispute over a particular amount of money.

A judgment lien applies if the plaintiff receives an award in his favor. The judgment lien immediately attaches to all real estate in your name and all bank accounts and brokerage accounts and other assets. A lien acts like a mortgage or trust deed. You cannot sell or refinance a property without paying off the creditor, and he can foreclose on the real estate and seize any accounts in your name. A creditor with a judgment lien clearly holds all of the cards. You have no leverage and no room to negotiate. At that point he has you. You are trapped, and there is no way out. Certainly that is not the position you want to be in when you deal with an adversary.

One of our clients, Ed, was a wealthy real estate investor and owned five apartment buildings worth about $3 million. Although he was involved in a lawsuit concerning a property dispute at the time, he believed he had little exposure. We set up a plan for him using several LLCs to hold the properties and a Privacy Trust to hold ownership in the LLCs. A year later we received a call from Ed telling us that he had lost the case, and there was a judgment against him for $1.5 million. Had he not set up the plan he would have been in big trouble. The plaintiff would have had a lien on all of Ed's real estate, worth $3 million, as security for the judgment. The property would have been frozen and then seized. The plaintiff would not have taken a penny less than the full amount of the judgment. Nothing to talk about or discuss—just pay up. That's a bad position to be in.

But because Ed was a smart guy, he was not in a bad position. Since all of his assets had been transferred into the plan, the judgment lien did not affect the properties. Ed was free to sell, refinance, collect rents, and deal with his property just as he had always done. Since the creditor had no security for his judgment and stood to collect nothing, Ed now had the leverage to negotiate a favorable settlement. He held all of the chips and, in fact, settled the case for $75,000—clearly a better result than losing the $1.5 million. In this case, the proper asset protection plan changed the relative bargaining power of each side. *Ed could have been weak and vulnerable but instead was able to negotiate from a position of superior strength.*

An architect client of ours had savings of about $75,000, which he had inherited from his mother. Architects have a high lawsuit risk, and he needed to protect these funds for the care and special education of his eight year old child who had severe physical and learning disabilities. Sure enough, within two years after setting up the plan, he was served with a lawsuit. The plaintiff attempted to get a pre-judgment attachment of the savings, but the judge ruled that the assets were properly protected within the LCC and could not be reached by a lien. Without any assurance of payment, the plaintiff's attorney quickly lost interest and the case was settled for under $2,000.

The importance of protecting valuable assets from pre-judgment attachments and judgment liens cannot be stressed enough. Without access to your funds, you can't pay your household expenses and you can't operate a business. Worse, if you can't pay your lawyer to defend the case, you will be forced into an immediate and unfavorable settlement. The proper strategy allows you to maintain access to your funds and your property during and after litigation. That's sound financial and business planning.

Tax Treatment of the LLC

All income of the LLC is passed directly through to the personal returns of the members. When property is transferred to the LLC or distributed from it, there are no separate tax consequences. Except in unusual circumstances, the general rule will apply and no gain or loss will be recognized on a contribution to or distribution from the company. There is no tax when funds are withdrawn from the company. The only tax paid is on the income earned, which is reported on the owner's personal tax return. This system avoids the complications and potential double taxation that plagues the corporate format.

Summary

In this chapter, we have discussed major benefits that can be accomplished with the LLC.

First, the LLC can be an important element of a plan that produces an excellent level of financial privacy. When an LLC is owned by a Privacy Trust, anonymous ownership of bank accounts, real estate investments, and business interests can be accomplished. Lawsuits and claims, which are based upon a knowledge of your personal financial matters, will be discouraged before they begin. When your assets are held with maximum privacy and confidentiality, a plaintiff or his lawyer looking for a Deep Pocket Defendant will not find any reachable assets when they investigate you. Since lawyers only sue if they believe they will be able to collect a judgment, using an effective plan will discourage most people from filing a lawsuit against you.

Second, if someone does file a lawsuit, we want to protect your assets from liens and attachments. Pre-judgment attachments are filed during a lawsuit and can freeze your real estate and bank accounts. Without access to funds to pay your personal and business expenses or to defend the case, you are, as they say, dead in the water. You will have no choice except to make a fast and unfavorable settlement—giving the plaintiff all or most of what he wants.

Similarly, a judgment lien will attach to all property that you own. You will be unable to sell, refinance, or collect rents on your property and all accounts will be seized. An asset protection plan will allow you to shield your property from liens and attachments during the lawsuit and after a judgment. Clearly this puts the negotiating chips on your side of the table and provides you with powerful leverage to create a successful result.

Third, Safe Assets such as your home and savings must be protected from the liability which can be caused by Dangerous Assets. There are hundreds of different ways for you to lose the nest egg that you have put together over many years of work. No matter what you do for a living, it will be hard to save up that money all over again. Sound planning allows you to insulate yourself from the potential liability of a Dangerous Asset. When risk is properly contained in this fashion you can proceed in the world with confidence that your savings will be secure and available when you need them.

CHAPTER EIGHT

Trusts for Asset Protection and Tax Savings

T HE ENTITY KNOWN as a *trust* will be essential in creating various strategies for accomplishing privacy, asset protection, and estate planning benefits. This chapter will provide a background for understanding how these techniques work.

The legal arrangement, known as a trust, has been around for at least several hundred years. Every trust has certain essential characteristics. A trust has one or more *trustees*, who are responsible for administering and carrying out the terms of the trust. The *beneficiaries* are those who are entitled to trust income or principle either currently or at some time in the future.

A trust is typically in the form of a written trust agreement between the *settlor*, the person creating the trust, and the trustee. The written trust agreement provides that the settlor will transfer certain assets to the trustee and the trustee will hold those assets for the benefit of the named beneficiaries. (The terms "trustor" or "grantor" are used interchangeably with the term "settlor.")

Until recently, trusts were used almost exclusively by the wealthiest families to maintain privacy and to pass their wealth to succeeding generations. The privacy benefits were particularly important. Grandpa Robber Baron had no desire to allow the muckraking newspapers and the antagonistic public to know exactly what he owned and how much he was worth. Grandpa was savvy enough to know that revealing the details of his fortune was not good for business and wasn't smart politics. The Vanderbilts, Whitneys, Rockefellers, and Carnegies created trusts which have now successfully shielded from public scrutiny the family wealth of five or more generations.

But it is no longer only the wealthy who are attracted to the powerful benefits offered by a properly designed trust. Now, those with equity in the family home or some savings put away for retirement or college are using trusts as an essential ingredient in their overall financial plan. Let's see how the different types of trusts can be used to accomplish your goals.

The Revocable Living Trust

A revocable living trust is a trust that can be revoked or canceled at any time by the settlor. The term "living trust" means simply that the trust is established during the lifetime of the settlor. (Testamentary trusts, those created upon the settlor's death, do not avoid probate and are not nearly as popular today as they once were.) During the past ten or fifteen years, revocable living trusts have gained enormous popularity as a sound technique for accomplishing a number of legitimate estate planning goals.

Avoiding Probate

A revocable trust (or irrevocable trust) that is properly drafted and funded will avoid probate. This is the most significant and valuable feature of a revocable trust. The benefits of avoiding probate can only be appreciated by understanding what happens when an estate must go through the probate process.

If a person dies owning property, not protected by a trust, a court will supervise the transfer of that property to those people named in his will. If someone dies without a will, his property passes to his relatives in the manner set forth under the laws of his state. The actual transfer of title to the decedent's property is carried out under the court's supervision by a person designated in the will as the Executor of the estate. If a person dies without a will, the court must appoint an Administrator to carry out the transfer of the decedent's property. An Executor or Administrator is known as a Personal Representative.

The Personal Representative has the responsibility to perform the following:

1. Locate, inventory, and appraise all of the assets of the decedent.

2. Make final payment to all of the decedent's creditors.

3. Prepare and file any federal and state death tax returns.

4. Distribute the assets of the decedent's estate according to the decedent's will or according to state law.

The Personal Representative will almost always hire an attorney to perform this work on his behalf. The attorneys collect their fees from the estate for these services. The amount of legal fees, depending upon the state, is either a fixed percentage of the estate or is based upon what a judge determines to be a reasonable fee.

The reason that most people do not want their estate to go through probate is that this process is expensive, time consuming, and inconvenient. Attorney's fees may range from 2 percent to 10 percent of the gross value of the estate. An estate of $1 million, depending upon the complications involved, may incur attorney's fees of $25,000. These fees are usually based upon the gross value of the estate rather than the net value. An estate of $1 million with $950,000 of liabilities might still pay attorney's fees of $25,000. But now this amount is 50 percent, not 2½ percent of the net value.

Second, attorneys rarely feel the same sense of urgency about completing the probate that is felt by the decedent's wife and children. While the decedent's family wishes to get on with things as quickly as possible, the attorney for the estate is often busy handling other matters and the time period for completing the probate may take from two to five years. Probate causes significant stress and frustration for the survivors, and avoiding the process is a legitimate planning concern.

Trustees and Beneficiaries

Revocable trusts are effective in avoiding probate only when the trust document has been properly drafted and only when all of the decedent's property has been transferred into the trust prior to his death. The trust document, like a will, provides for the disposition of trust assets upon the death of the settlor. In the typical arrangement, a husband and wife will create a revocable trust with both husband and wife as the initial trustees. They are also the beneficiaries of the trust. The trust provides that during their joint lifetimes the trust may be revoked at any time. Upon the death of either spouse, the trust typically becomes irrevocable and the surviving spouse becomes the sole trustee. When the surviving spouse dies, the trust property passes according to the wishes expressed in the trust document.

Funding the Trust

For the revocable trust to be effective in eliminating probate, it is essential that all family assets be transferred into the trust prior to a spouse's death. Any property that has not been transferred into the trust will be subject to probate, defeating the purpose of creating it in the first place. An amazing number of people go to the trouble and expense of forming a revocable trust and then fail to complete the work necessary to fund it.

Funding the trust involves transferring legal title from husband and wife into the name of the trust. For example, if Harry and Martha Jones are funding their revocable trust, they will change title to their assets from "Harry Jones and Martha Jones, husband and wife" to "Harry Jones and Martha Jones as Trustees of the Jones Family Trust, Dated January 1, 1999."

For real estate, the change in title is accomplished by executing and recording a deed to the property. Bank accounts and brokerage accounts can be transferred by simply changing the name on the accounts to reflect the trust as the new owner. Shares of stock and bonds in registered form are changed by notifying the transfer agent for the issuing company and requesting that the certificates be reissued in the name of the trust. Stock in a family owned corporation can be changed by endorsing the old stock certificate to the trust and having the corporation issue a new certificate to the trust. Other types of property can be transferred by a simple written declaration called an Assignment.

The living trust also can be funded indirectly by transferring interests in other entities. For example, if you hold your property in a Family Limited Partnership or Limited Liability Company, the living trust can hold your shares in those companies. In our discussion of the Privacy Trust, we will see how this can be a useful strategy for privacy and asset protection.

Estate Taxes

The trust must also contain the appropriate provisions in order to minimize federal taxes payable upon the death of either spouse. It is important to point out that estate taxes can be minimized with either a properly drawn will or a properly drawn revocable trust. The revocable trust does not provide any tax advantages that are not available to a person using a will or some other form of trust in order to accomplish a transfer of his property. But as long as you are using this type of trust to avoid probate and to take advantage of its unique features, you should make sure that the estate tax provisions are properly handled.

Federal taxes are imposed on most transfers of property during your lifetime or at the time of your death. Prior to 1977, estate taxes for transfers at death were distinct from gift taxes that were applied to transfers of property during lifetime. The gift tax rate was 75 percent of the estate tax rate. In 1977, this dual rate structure was abolished and a uniform rate was established for both gift and estate tax purposes. As a result of this change and additional changes in 1981 and 1996, there is an effective tax exemption of $650,000 (effective in 1999) for transfers during life or at death. (We will refer to this amount as the exemption amount.) Amounts in excess of the exemption amount are taxed at rates ranging from 37 percent to a maximum of 50 percent for total transfers exceeding $2.5 million. The exemption amount will increase incrementally until in reaches $1 million in 2006.

The law provides that annual gifts of $10,000 and under are excluded from tax. A husband and wife together can give $20,000 per year. This amount applies to each person to whom a gift is made. A husband and wife could give, as an example, a total of $100,000 per year to their five children and grandchildren.

Further, the 1981 law adopted a provision known as the Unlimited Marital Deduction. All amounts transferred between husband and wife, during lifetime or at death, are exempt from tax. This means that if a husband leaves all of his property to his surviving spouse, there will be no estate taxes on his death regardless of the size of his estate. The estate taxes will arise on the death of the second spouse, as she transfers her property to her children or other relatives.

Minimizing Taxes

The unified tax credit allows each spouse to transfer up to the exemption amount to his children (or anyone else) free of any federal estate taxes. In its simplest form, a properly drawn revocable trust takes advantage of this benefit by providing for the creation of two separate trusts on the death of the first spouse. These two trusts are referred to as the A trust and the B trust.

In a large estate, the B trust will be funded with the exemption amount and the balance will go into the A trust. From the A trust, the surviving spouse will have the right to all income for life plus a power to use any portion of the principal that he or she so desires. The B trust will generally provide that the surviving spouse is entitled to all income during his or her life plus the right to use principal for health, education, maintenance, and support.

Any amount left in the A trust, in excess of the exemption amount, at the death of the surviving spouse will be taxable in his or her estate for estate tax purposes. However, since the surviving spouse is given only limited rights over the B trust, the amount in the B trust will not be taxable in the survivor's estate upon his or her death. The effect of these provisions is that the spouses' combined exemption amount (ultimately $2 million) can be passed

from husband and wife to their beneficiaries without being subject to estate taxes.

Income Tax Treatment
of Revocable Trusts

During one's lifetime, revocable trusts do not provide any income
tax savings. For tax purposes, the trusts are treated as if they do
not exist. A revocable trust is known, for tax purposes, as a grantor
trust. A grantor trust is not a taxpaying entity. No annual tax return is required to be filed. Instead, all income and loss of the trust
is reported on the tax returns of the husband and wife.

Revocable Trusts and
Asset Protection

A revocable trust does not provide any protection of assets from
judgment creditors. It is ignored for creditor purposes just as it is
ignored for income tax purposes. In most states, the law provides
that if a settlor has the right to revoke the trust, all of the assets are
treated as owned by the settlor. Perhaps because of the promotion
associated with these trusts, many people mistakenly believe that
a revocable trust somehow shields assets from creditors. This is
not correct. If there is a judgment against you, the creditor is entitled to seize any assets that you have in the trust.

Asset protection can be accomplished when property is held in
the FLP or LLC and those interests are owned by the trust. We
will look at this arrangement in detail in the next chapter.

Gifts Between Spouses

As we have stated, gifts between spouses qualify for the Unlimited
Marital Deduction which eliminates federal gift taxes on these kinds
of transfers. The ability to shift the ownership of property be-

tween husband and wife without creating a tax liability creates some useful opportunities for achieving valuable asset protection.

Community Property

In community property states, each spouse's interest in the community property is subject to the claims of the other spouse's creditors. If there is a judgment against the husband, all community property assets held by husband and wife are available to satisfy the judgment. On the other hand, the separate property of a spouse will generally not be subject to the claims of the creditors of the other spouse.

These rules provide some obvious opportunities to achieve a measure of asset protection. If community property is divided into equal shares of separate property of the husband and separate property of the wife, those separate property interests will not be available to satisfy the claims of the other spouse's creditor. Generally, a living trust would be created for each spouse—for the estate planning benefits and to confirm that the marital property has been divided. Those in community property states can at least limit their potential exposure to a creditor's claim to one-half of the marital property, rather than all of the marital property, by creating this type of division.

The primary drawback of this technique is that a division of community property into separate property trusts may be disadvantageous from an income tax standpoint. All property held as community property receives a stepped-up basis on the death of the first spouse. For example, a husband and wife buy a property during their marriage for $50,000 that is later worth $100,000. If they sell the property, they will have a gain of $50,000 and will pay taxes on that amount. Suppose that instead of selling, the property is held until the time the first spouse dies. All community property now receives a new tax basis equal to its value as of the date of death—$100,000 in this example. Therefore, if the property is held until the death of the first spouse, all taxable gain is eliminated.

This favorable situation does not occur when a husband and wife hold separate property. In this situation, only the deceased spouse's interest in the property receives the stepped-up basis. In the above example, if the property were held one-half each by Husband and Wife, only the interest of the deceased spouse would receive the new basis. This would result in a $75,000 basis, and a $25,000 gain, if the surviving spouse sold the property for $100,000.

If you hold community property that has substantially appreciated in value, it probably would not be advisable to divide the property into separate shares and thereby lose out on the significant tax savings that can otherwise be achieved. Alternative methods of asset protection should be explored.

Separate Property

■ Unequal Division of Property

For those living in states which do not recognize community property, gifts of separate property between a husband and wife can achieve some useful asset protection.

If one spouse is more vulnerable to potential lawsuits than the other spouse, property can simply be transferred by gift from that spouse to a living trust for the other. For example, if the husband is a physician with a high vulnerability to lawsuits and the wife is a school teacher with low lawsuit vulnerability, property can be transferred by gift from Husband to Wife's living trust to reduce the amount of assets subject to loss in the event of a lawsuit. In theory, all assets could be moved out of the name of Husband and into the name of Wife's trust. In the event of a subsequent lawsuit and judgment against the husband, no assets would be available to satisfy the creditor.

The advantage of this gift technique is that it is simple and inexpensive to utilize. Gifts between spouses do not create any gift tax liability because of the unlimited marital deductions for gifts between spouses.

One problem with this technique is that, in many cases, a spouse will be reluctant to relinquish all effective control over his property. If all family assets, including real estate and bank accounts are in the sole name of the wife's living trust, the husband may not feel comfortable with this arrangement. The threat of a potential lawsuit at some future time will rarely be sufficient to overcome the desire to maintain at least equal management and control over one's property.

Along these lines, in the event of a divorce, a court may be unwilling to rearrange any bona-fide transfers previously made between spouses. Although a court in a dissolution proceeding has broad equitable powers to divide marital assets in a fair and just manner, property which was the subject of a bona-fide gift from a husband to his wife may or may not be reallocated by a judge. In our practice, we have found that many clients are not willing to risk the possibility that they will be permanently deprived of assets previously transferred to the other spouse.

Lastly, despite the fact that the wife has a low level of lawsuit vulnerability associated with her work, the fact remains that there are numerous ways she could still be sued. Remember, as the owner of substantial assets, she becomes an inviting target for a lawsuit. Putting all of your eggs in this basket is a dangerous proposition.

■ Equal Division of Property

An equal division of marital property, as opposed to a strict transfer from one spouse to the other, might provide greater lawsuit protection and might also allow each spouse to sleep more easily. Marital property can be divided according to a written agreement which states that each spouse is to hold one-half of all marital property as their own separate property. This is where a revocable trust may become particularly useful for our purposes. Once the marital property is divided, two separate revocable trusts can be established, one for each spouse. The husband's trust then holds title to his one-half of the property, and the wife's trust holds title to her one-half interest.

When marital property is divided in this manner, a number of our previous concerns are eliminated. First, when property is held pursuant to a written trust agreement, it is unlikely that a court would imply the existence of some other type of trust arrangement that is not consistent with the terms of the written trust. It is unlikely that a court would allow a creditor of the husband to reach into and claim the property held in the wife's revocable trust on the theory that she is holding that property for the benefit of her husband. As a result, property held by the wife in her trust would be immune to potential claims from the husband's creditors. Although the property in the husband's trust would still be available for these creditors' claims, at least one-half of the total estate has been removed from the reach of the husband's creditors. Admittedly this is only a partial solution to the problem, but it is a useful beginning.

This arrangement also minimizes concerns about losing management and control over one's assets. The husband would still have full management and control over the assets in his revocable trust and, in the event of a divorce, each spouse is likely to have no more property than they would otherwise be entitled to.

Gifts to Family Members

Making gifts of property to family members is a useful tool that may accomplish a variety of asset protection and estate panning objectives. A properly structured program of gift giving, to one's children or grandchildren, can result in a minimization of estate and income taxes and can also be useful for achieving a significant degree of lawsuit protection.

There are significant tax advantages to a gift giving program. Lifetime gifts reduce the size of one's estate and consequently minimize the ultimate amount of estate taxes. Since estate tax rates are high, substantial savings will be realized from this technique.

A gift giving program may also produce some annual income tax savings. If a donee is fourteen years or older, income earned on the property transferred to him will be taxable to the child rather than to the parent. If a child is in a lower income tax bracket than the parent, a gift program will effectively spread the income tax liability of the family among lower bracket taxpayers and will thereby reduce the overall income tax burden.

A gift program also provides significant lawsuit protection. If a gift transfer does not violate the fraudulent conveyance laws, property that has been transferred to a child or a grandchild cannot be reached by a judgment creditor of the husband or wife. Once an effective gift has been made from a parent to a child, this asset cannot be seized by the parents' creditors.

Drawbacks of Outright Gifts

The most obvious difficulty with outright gifts is the total loss of ownership and control of the gifted property. In our years of legal practice, we have rarely encountered instances in which parents are willing to transfer complete control over large sums of money to their children. Despite considerable estate and income tax savings, few people are willing to give up a portion of their wealth which they have worked hard to accumulate during their lifetime.

Even when their wealth is beyond what they reasonably need to live comfortably, parents are concerned about the wisdom of making outright gifts to their children. Sometimes there is an issue concerning the child's marital status and what will happen to the gifted property in the event the child is divorced. Sometimes there are concerns about the child's level of financial responsibility and whether the funds will be squandered. Many times the parents are concerned about the creditors of a child reaching the property. When the situation involves minor children or grandchildren, who are not legally capable of holding title to property, there are questions about who will act on the child's behalf in holding the property and when the property should be distributed to the child. These are all matters of great consequence and must be carefully considered by parents contemplating this type of gift giving program.

Irrevocable Trusts

Some additional problems of an outright gift giving program can be eliminated or mitigated through the use of an irrevocable trust. This technique also opens up a world of planning possibilities for privacy, asset protection and tax planning strategies which we will explore in detail in chapter 9.

The distinguishing feature of an irrevocable trust is, as the name implies, that the trust cannot be revoked or canceled by the settlor. The irrevocable trust is a written agreement between the settlor and the trustee in which the trustee agrees to hold property transferred by the settlor on behalf of certain specified beneficiaries.

Typically, the beneficiaries will be the children or grandchildren. The parents may transfer to the trust the annual exclusion amount of $20,000 per year for each beneficiary. If the parents' estate is large enough and they can afford to do so, they may make a larger gift, using all or a portion of their combined exemption amount of up to $2 million. The greater the amount of the gift, the more significant the estate tax, income tax, and lawsuit protection achievements.

Gift Tax Consequences

If the transfer to the trust is considered to be a *completed gift*, it may give rise to current gift tax liability should the value of the gift exceed the exemption amount. A husband and wife may use up their combined credits against tax without incurring any immediate tax liability. And, as discussed, additional annual transfers with a value of $20,000 per donee can be made. If you own property with a value greater than the exemption amount, it may be difficult to make an immediate transfer of all of the property to a trust without triggering a gift tax liability. Often, the Family Limited Partnership is used to avoid gift tax by creating a discounted value for the property as we discussed in chapter 6.

Incomplete Gifts

To transfer amounts over the exemption amount without gift tax, a trust arrangement can be created which is not considered to be a completed gift for gift tax purposes. Although the trust is irrevocable and the transfer is complete under state law with respect to potential creditors, a gift can still be incomplete for tax purposes. An incomplete gift occurs when the donor retains some significant powers over the gifted property. Even if the donor cannot reacquire the property and cannot enjoy the property himself, if he is able to exercise significant control over the property, the gift will be considered incomplete.

For example, if a donor retains a right to add beneficiaries to the trust or to alter the interests of the beneficiaries, the transfer would not be a completed gift and no gift tax liability would be created. Similarly, for income tax purposes, the trust can be structured so that all of the income tax attributes of the property are retained by the donor. In essence, the trust would be treated as a *grantor trust*, in the same manner as the revocable trust. If you wish to protect certain property, without incurring any gift tax liability, the incomplete gift technique is an excellent method for doing so.

Advantages of the Irrevocable Trust

The irrevocable trust solves a number of problems posed by the outright gift giving program. If you are the trustee, even if you have transferred substantial assets into the trust, you will still enjoy the management and control over that property. Although the trustee cannot use the property for his own benefit, he may retain some degree of discretion regarding the investment of trust assets and the amount and timing of any distributions to the beneficiaries. This ability to maintain effective control over the transferred property will alleviate one of the most frequent concerns.

Second, a child's interest in this kind of trust can be protected from the child's spouse in the event of a divorce, or from creditors in the event of a judgment. Although the outcome on these issues depends in part upon the law in your particular state and the language which is used in drafting the trust agreement, protection from spouses and potential creditors is a major advantage which can be accomplished using the irrevocable trust.

The third advantage is that the trust mechanism allows gifts to be made to minor children or grandchildren. Since minors cannot hold the property in their own name, the use of a trust is essential in order to provide them with the benefits of property ownership and to accomplish the gift program.

Tax Savings and
Lawsuit Protection

Property which has been transferred to the trust by gift will not be included in the parents' estate when they die—if the initial transfer was a completed gift. If the transfers begin early enough and continue over a period of years, a significant amount of estate tax savings can be realized. If the parents have, for example, five children and grandchildren, a total of $100,000 per year can be transferred into an irrevocable trust without gift tax consequences. Over a ten-year period, $1 million has been removed from the parents' estate. If the parents are in a maximum estate tax bracket of 50 percent, a total of $500,000 in family wealth will be preserved.

Income tax savings also can be achieved when the beneficiaries are in a lower tax bracket than the parents and are fourteen years or older. Although an irrevocable trust is a separate taxpaying entity, apart from the parents, income which is distributed from the trust to a beneficiary is taxable to the beneficiary. If the parents are in the maximum effective tax bracket and the trust beneficiaries are in lower tax brackets, annual income tax savings can be accomplished through this difference in the tax rates. Over a period of time, this annual tax savings can add up to a substantial amount of money.

The irrevocable trust also provides a significant degree of lawsuit protection for the parents. Because the trust is irrevocable and cannot be canceled or modified in any manner by the parent, and because the parents have no interest in the trust as beneficiaries, property that has been transferred to the trust will be protected from the claims of the parents' creditors.

Factors to Consider

In deciding whether to use an irrevocable trust to accomplish these objectives, there are two primary factors that must be considered. First, this trust cannot be revoked, altered, or modified in any manner. Once the parents have transferred property into the trust, it cannot be retrieved. If the financial circumstances of the parents change in the future, they still will not be able to reach the property. The parents must ask themselves: "How much can I afford to transfer?" and "How much do I need to keep to meet my personal needs during my lifetime?" Clearly, if the parents transfer all of their assets into the irrevocable trust, the parents must have sufficient income from other sources meet their own needs.

Within the last few years, several states have adopted legislation that eases the traditional restrictions on irrevocable trusts. In particular, Alaska and Delaware have passed laws allowing individuals to create trusts which provide asset protection, privacy, and estate planning benefits—while retaining the right to income or principal. In effect, these states are offering the advantages traditionally reserved for offshore trusts, within a domestic framework. Because these arrangements are still new, we do not yet know how successful these trusts will be. For now, they present interesting planning opportunities, and future developments should be carefully studied.

Summary

The legal arrangement known as a trust is the foundation of every sound estate plan. The threat of loss from lawsuits, estate taxes, probate costs, and privacy intrusions can be effectively minimized with a trust designed to accomplish that purpose. In the next chapter, we will see how the Privacy Trust builds upon the traditional techniques and the latest developments to protect accumulated wealth from a variety of perils.

CHAPTER NINE

The
Privacy Trust

The Privacy Trust

T HE PRIVACY TRUST is a descriptive name for the legal strategies designed to achieve financial privacy goals. The Privacy Trust successfully conceals ownership of bank and brokerage accounts, the family home, rental properties, and interests in other entities. If you have established a corporation, Family Limited Partnership, or Limited Liability Company for business or asset protection purposes, the Privacy Trust adds a desirable level of confidentiality to your personal affairs. Depending upon the particular features included in the trust—in addition to the privacy advantages— formidable asset protection and estate planning benefits can be created.

Creating Legal Privacy

Legal privacy for financial matters is a scarce and valuable commodity. As we have discussed, developments in technology now allow powerful search engines to sort through billions of records stored in vast interconnected databases. These programs are capable of locating and assembling disparate facts about your life into a comprehensive personal information report with detailed background, credit, employment, and financial information. The ready availability of bank and brokerage account balances and real estate ownership provides a potential adversary with an accurate picture of sensitive personal matters that you would choose not to disclose.

The full extent of the dangers associated with these privacy intrusions is only now becoming apparent. The Federal Bureau of Investigation reports that identity theft is the fastest growing crime in the nation. Easy access to personal identifying information such as name, address, birth date, Social Security number, and driver's license number allows a third party to pose as the victim, run up credit card bills, take out loans and mortgages, and open fraudulent bank accounts. An enterprising individual or an organized ring using hundreds of stolen identities can make millions of dollars within a few months and then disappear before the victims have even learned of the crime. The victims are left with collection actions, judgments, and devastated credit that may be impossible to repair. Congress has responded to these particular abuses with the Identity Theft and Deterrence Act of 1998, which provides criminal penalties for identity theft and gives victims the right to seek restitution from the perpetrators.

Identity theft is an easy and profitable crime, and the threat of prosecution is not likely to discourage these types of activities. Your key personal identifying information—such as Social Security number, date and place of birth, and mother's maiden name—has already been distributed so widely that it cannot be retrieved. Privacy rights groups will advise you not to give out this information anymore, but it is too late for that. If you tear up your credit cards, refuse to fill out surveys, hang up on telephone solicitors and keep out of the newspapers, your information may eventually fade from view. As your name appears less frequently on the computer generated lists of affluent, creditworthy individuals, you might decrease your chances of being noticed and selected by an identity thief. But there is no practical way to remove yourself from the system. The volumes of information about you in the databases of the credit reporting agencies, public records, and information vendors don't belong to you. They belong to the companies that compile the information, and you can't restrict the flow of what is already out there.

It is possible and advisable to limit the availability of certain types of financial information about yourself. Although a variety of regulatory and reporting requirements create obstacles, the ownership of assets can be shielded from public disclosure. As long as taxes are paid on the income earned and the techniques are not used to conceal the proceeds of criminal activities, anonymous ownership can be legal and effective. Dangers associated with predatory lawsuits and threats from potential adversaries can be successfully combated by adopting strategies which defeat the information gathering processes.

Limiting the Supply of Personal Information

The success of a strategy to keep your financial assets secret depends upon the same premise as the rest of your secrets in life. The fewer people that know something about you—the better. And those few people who know should be very good at keeping it to themselves.

Let's see how this principle applies when you open a bank account. You would like to keep the existence of the account, your balances, and your transactions confidential. The representative who opens your account assures you that the bank maintains strict privacy standards and would never disclose customer information to anyone. The account opening agreement requests your name, address, date and place of birth, driver's license number, and your Social Security number. This information is entered into the bank's computer and an account number is assigned. What level of privacy should you now expect?

The account information in the bank computer is now available throughout all of the bank branches to virtually every employee. Account information is maintained centrally and is accessed through the terminals of every teller, loan officer, and customer service representative by a search under your name, account number, or Social Security number. The merger trend in the financial services industry makes ever larger quantities of customer information available to a greater number of people. Bank of America recently completed a merger with Nationsbank to create the largest bank in the country with 4,854 branches, 30 million customers, and 200,000 employees.

With access to personal account information available to so many employees, the financial institutions cannot control the flow of customer information from the bank to the outside. The investigators and information brokers who seek account information for clients on a regular basis pay bank employees to supply individual accounts records. So the first problem you have with your account secrecy is that even if the bank wanted to protect your privacy, it would have a difficult time preventing disclosure by its employees.

Your second problem is that when your bank tells you that it values your privacy, that doesn't mean what you think it does. It really means that the information about your account is *valuable to the bank*. Sophisticated databases allow financial firms to create intimate profiles of customer portfolios, savings, and spending habits. This information is then used by the firm—or an outside marketing company—to create highly selective and targeted presentations to sell you services and products. Information about you and your account activity is a prime source of revenue for the firm, and it is exploited, traded, and sold like any other asset.

The recent merger between Citicorp and Travelers Group Inc., (now called Citigroup) illustrates this point. The plan is intended to create the world's largest "financial supermarket" with nearly 700 billion dollars in assets. Products would be cross-sold to what were, previously, each other's customers based upon the information gathered by each division. The combined company includes 10,300 stockbrokers at the Salomon Smith Barney subsidiary and 180,000 full- and part-time insurance salespeople. Detailed account information and behavioral analyses of bank customers will allow the new sales force to individually tailor each pitch for annuities, mutual funds, and insurance products.

Imagine the potential. A broker from the Salomon Smith Barney division of Citigroup calls Mrs. Wilson about her $100,000 certificate of deposit at Citicorp which is about to come due. Although the two have had no previous business relationship, he tells her that he is calling from her bank and, as a service to its valued customers, has been asked to perform a thorough financial analysis of her account. After weighing the available investment options, his recommendation is that she purchase a Citigroup variable annuity with her $100,000 savings. Or he might suggest putting her savings in the stock market, or in a mutual fund, or perhaps purchasing life insurance—anything to shift her out of the low margin CD and into a high profit, big commission insurance or investment product.

Citicorp lures the customers with the convenience of thousands of branch offices, ATMs, and online banking. It might even be willing to pay higher interest rates on CDs and deposits—a loss leader—simply to attract additional accounts. Once you are a customer, your individual customer data is gathered, spending and saving patterns and available cash are processed and analyzed, and the information is turned over to the sales force. Then the real money is made by selling investments and insurance products loaded with fat fees and commissions.

This example is an accurate portrayal of the tactics that are used by the financial firms. NationsBank (now merged with Bank of America) signed a consent decree with the Securities and Exchange Commission agreeing to stop misrepresenting the safety of certain investments offered to its customers. The bank had provided its sales force with customer lists of maturing CDs—together with financial statements and account balances for likely prospects. The customers—many of whom had never invested in anything other than CDs—were told to switch their money into an investment called a "Term Trust," which "were as safe as CDs but better because they paid more." In reality, these Term Trusts were pools of funds that were invested in high risk derivatives and which proceeded to lose much of the customer's money. The consent decree does not bar the company from using customer account information to sell products, it merely prohibits misleading statements about the products.

The use of account information to sell products is not limited to these examples. Every company in the industry has recognized the effectiveness of the strategy and is scrambling to create marketing alliances, joint ventures, and mergers with others to acquire product lines and sales forces. The days of the small, independent local bank are gone forever. The little guys cannot remain competitive without large capital investments in technology and marketing, and so they are gobbled up by the regional and national firms. In San Diego, where we live, only one independent bank remains. Union Bank, Wells Fargo, Bank of America, and Washington Mutual have acquired every other local bank.

Now that you have the broad picture about how the financial firms operate, what conclusions can we reach about the secrecy of your account? We know that the information is widely available to employees and is traded and distributed by the firm to inside and outside sales forces. If you hope to accomplish secrecy by restricting access to particular information, it is easy to see that this ambition will be defeated from the very instant that the account is opened. As your account information is keyed into the computer, it is turned into a digital packet and shipped into the stream of commerce. To state the matter most directly, you can expect that all information in the possession of the financial firm will be available to anyone who wants it, for whatever reason.

What the Privacy Trust Achieves

The approach we have developed is to hold all financial accounts within the Privacy Trust. This legal arrangement prevents the firm from acquiring any useful personal information. Since financial firms are not good at keeping secrets, we just won't tell them anything. The Privacy Trust acts as an intermediary to remove the connection between you and the account. Neither your name, nor your Social Security number, nor any other personal identifying information appears in any records related to your account. No employees of the firm are aware of your relationship to the account, and the bank can't sell information that it doesn't have. That's the proper model for creating financial privacy.

Information about your real estate assets—your home and other property can also be shielded from public disclosure. Since these records are publicly recorded and can be gathered through a database search—privacy means severing the connection between you and the property. When the records are searched under your name or identifying information, you do not want your home and other properties to appear on the list. If you hold real estate in a corporation, FLP, or LLC, your ownership of these entities must be concealed as part of any privacy strategy. Locating your property and determining its value is the easiest and most popular technique for measuring your attractiveness as a potential target for litigation or any other type of claim.

The Privacy Trust can be created in a simple and straightforward manner to accomplish most privacy, asset protection, and estate planning objectives. Progressive levels of sophistication can be added as the complexity of the financial circumstances increase. Advanced planning strategies may include a variety of domestic or offshore options, depending upon the particular results to be accomplished. For descriptive purposes, we can divide the Privacy Trust into Plan #1 and Plan #2, which we will discuss in this chapter; and Plan #3, held for the next chapter. We base the distinctions upon the key privacy and asset protection feature of each.

Privacy Trust–Plan #1
Anonymous Ownership

The Privacy Trust–Plan #1 is a convenient and flexible arrangement that successfully conceals ownership of a variety of assets. As its name clearly states, it is used specifically for the purpose of avoiding public disclosure of real estate, financial accounts, and personal property. This trust is commonly used by celebrities and public figures to hold title to the family residence, vacation homes, and investment accounts.

The Role of the Trustee

The feature that creates the ability to achieve privacy for these assets is the use of a special type of corporate trustee—whose duties are to carry out your instructions. The corporate trustee does not invest or manage trust assets. His role is strictly limited to acting as your agent and nominee and executing documents as you request.

This role differs significantly from that of a typical trustee. The responsibilities are, likewise, dissimilar from the traditional responsibilities assumed by a trustee. Most trust companies are in business to manage assets—and they charge substantial fees for performing these services. The company makes investment decisions for the trust and distributes funds according to the terms of the trust agreement. Specific requests by the settlor or the beneficiaries must be reviewed by trust officers and their counsel to make sure that legal responsibilities and fiduciary duties are satisfied. Within this bureaucratic structure, even relatively simple matters are time consuming and expensive to accomplish. Although these traditional trust services can be useful for a client who needs extensive independent asset management for an elderly or minor beneficiary, that is not the type of arrangement that most of our clients prefer.

Instead, our clients who create a Privacy Trust generally want to maintain control and authority over their property—while using the trust company only for the limited purpose of holding legal title and executing necessary documents as instructed. The requirements for the trust company are:

1. It must be adequately capitalized and bonded to assure the safety of trust assets.

2. It must be licensed and regulated by state banking authorities.

3. Trust officers at the company must have authority to respond quickly and efficiently to all instructions from the settlor.

When the proper precautions are taken to guarantee the safety of the property and we are satisfied that the trust company will carry out directions in a timely manner, the Privacy Trust can be created.

Why This Plan Works

In the typical arrangement, the trust agreement specifies that you—as the settlor—have the right to revoke the trust at any time and that the trustee will perform only those activities specifically directed by you. Real estate is acquired or transferred into the name of the trust and financial accounts are opened at the bank or brokerage firm you choose.

The name on the property and the accounts is changed from your name to the name of the trust. For example, if we use the ABC Trust Company, the name of the trust could be ABC Trust #4006. Title to your home or other real estate is removed from your name and simply reads ABC Trust #4006. The trustee acts on your behalf for executing purchase or loan documents. Many lenders are familiar with these types of trusts and are comfortable with a mortgage loan in the name of the trust. You are required to maintain and manage the property in the trust. The trustee holds legal title for your benefit, but your responsibilities are not diminished.

An account at a bank or brokerage firm can also be opened in the name of ABC Trust #4006. The account opening agreement and the signature card are signed by the Trust Company. The tax identification number of the Trust Company is furnished. Your name and identifying information are not supplied to the financial firm—there is no visible connection between you and the trust.

This arrangement creates a true model for privacy because the financial firm and its employees *do not know* that you are the true owner of the account. Any inquiries regarding an account under your name or Social Security number will come up empty. They can't give away secrets they don't know. Your name is not in the computer and, as far as they know, you don't exist. The computer can apply sophisticated software analysis to the account to track savings and investment activity, and the firm can devise perfect product fits based upon the patterns evidenced in your account. But the firm can't sell your information, or give it to its sales force because the firm doesn't have a name behind the account. Now you control access to your personal information. It belongs to you and not the bank, and you can control what you supply to the outside world.

Sam, a private investigator, is contacted by attorney Aardvark who wants to know if you have enough assets to make it worthwhile to sue you. Sam flips on his computer, pours a cup of coffee, and dials into the database service that searches nationwide for real estate ownership. He keys in your name and Social Security number, but the screen says "No Matching Files Were Found." Your home and vacation house in the name of ABC Trust #4006 are not located in the search. Next, Sam contacts the agency that provides searches for bank and brokerage accounts and again—no luck. Since there is no record linking you to the trust account, a computer search of the customer accounts at every firm will produce no successful hits. At this point—with no real estate or financial accounts—he calls the attorney and tells him to find a better lawsuit prospect.

This strategy successfully protects the privacy of your sensitive financial information by strictly limiting the access. The information is secure because it is not made available to the bank, its thousands of employees, and its sales force. In contrast to your bank, the trust company has a legal and contractual obligation to maintain the confidentiality of the trust. It is in the business of providing fiduciary services and cannot breach the trust agreement without serious legal ramifications. It is certainly true that if somebody wants information badly enough they can penetrate any source. But a trust company with the proper safeguards in place will seriously reduce the risk of unauthorized disclosure.

In addition to the privacy benefits, all of the typical estate planning advantages can be achieved. The trust will perform the same role as a living trust to avoid probate, minimize estate taxes, and pass your property according to your wishes.

In the Privacy Trust–Plan #1, assets are owned directly by the trust as diagrammed in figure 9-1.

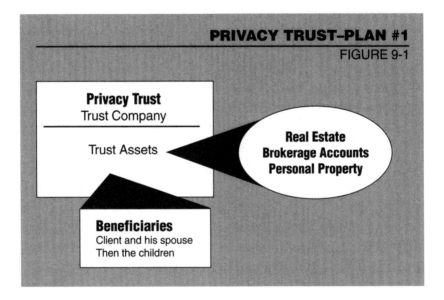

PRIVACY TRUST–PLAN #1

FIGURE 9-1

Privacy Trust
Trust Company

Trust Assets

Real Estate
Brokerage Accounts
Personal Property

Beneficiaries
Client and his spouse
Then the children

Who Should Use This Plan

This arrangement is used most often by individuals who are primarily concerned with financial privacy issues. A client of ours had an elderly mother whose assets consisted of $200,000 in savings at a brokerage firm. We put the funds in a Privacy Trust specifically for the purpose of eliminating high pressure telemarketing pitches for investment products and phony investment schemes. Our client wanted to protect against the risk that his mother would lose her money to a scam artist using account information to victimize the elderly.

We also have created this type of Privacy Trust for several clients in law enforcement—police officers and federal agents—who want to avoid privacy intrusions from dangerous individuals they have dealt with in their line of work. Similarly, for entertainers and public officials, who are well known by the public, we are often asked to conceal ownership of their homes and financial holdings with the use of this particular technique.

The Privacy Trust–Plan #1 is not designed to protect the assets of the trust from a judgment or a claim against you. Since the trust is revocable, the law provides that property in the trust can be reached in a collection proceeding. Although most lawsuits will be discouraged by the secrecy attributes, if you own Dangerous Assets or have substantial liability risks from your business you should consider a strategy which combines asset protection features with the Privacy Trust.

Privacy Trust–Plan #2
Asset Protection Plus Privacy

The Privacy Trust–Plan #2 adds the asset protection benefits to the plan which we have just described. When we supplement the trust with an entity such as a corporation, Family Limited Partnership, or Limited Liability Company, we can insulate and shield assets from the risks of potential liability. Rather than holding property directly in the trust, we hold assets within entities that are designed to accomplish asset protection purposes. The interests in those entities are owned by the trust.

How to Use Plan–#2

Here's an illustration of a typical plan. Our client, Henry, is married with three small children. He owns a dry cleaning business and a four-unit apartment building. These assets represent his lifetime savings. Henry and his wife want a plan to achieve three major goals:

1. **Privacy**—An important goal is anonymous ownership of the business and the real estate. During the previous ten years, Henry has been named in six frivolous lawsuits from customers, employees, and tenants. Although he won in court each time, the legal fees and the worry associated with the litigation have taken a financial and emotional toll.

2. **Protecting Family Savings**—The business and the real estate are both Dangerous Assets. A liability produced by either could wipe out all of the equity in the other. Henry wants a plan to ensure that if something goes wrong with the business or the property, he will not lose all of his savings.

3. **Estate Planning**—Avoiding probate, minimizing taxes, and providing for the care and support of his minor children are the remaining objectives of Henry's overall plan.

Each of Henry's concerns can be addressed within the convenient strategy of the Privacy Trust–Plan #2.

Let's see how this plan, depicted in figure 9-2, accomplishes Henry's goals.

We transferred the dry cleaning business into a Limited Liability Company (LLC #1) and gave the trust 100 percent of the interests in the LLC. Henry's name no longer appears as the owner. Licenses and permits are in the name of the company, and the

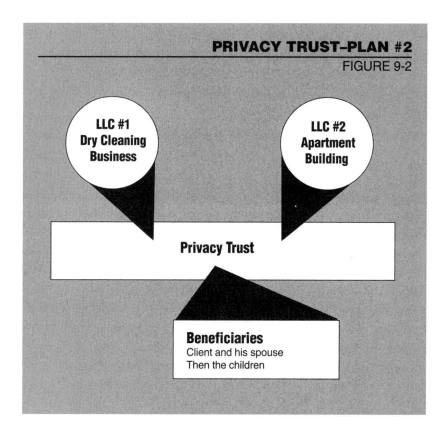

PRIVACY TRUST–PLAN #2
FIGURE 9-2

LLC #1
Dry Cleaning
Business

LLC #2
Apartment
Building

Privacy Trust

Beneficiaries
Client and his spouse
Then the children

public filing shows that the LLC is the owner of the business. The Articles of Organization for the LLC list the name of the trust—but not Henry's name. The same plan was followed for the apartment building. A deed transferred title to the apartment building into LLC #2. Anyone attempting to discern the owner of the LLC would find only the name of the trust. Important privacy goals have been achieved.

This strategy also provides a high level of asset protection. The LLC creates a legal shield, which protects each asset from a liability generated by the other. Henry can operate the dry cleaning business in LLC #1 without concern about being named in a lawsuit and without jeopardizing the apartment building. Similarly, liability from the property will be contained in LLC #2 without risk to the business.

Additional protection is furnished because a judgment creditor cannot seize the assets of either LLC. If there is a lawsuit against Henry for an unexpected reason, the business and the real estate—secure in the LLCs—are insulated from the claim. Although the membership interests held by the trust are subject to a charging order, this remedy is generally not effective and is unlikely to be pursued by a plaintiff.

A variety of estate planning features are easily integrated into this plan. The Privacy Trust has provisions that allow Henry's wife to continue the management of the family assets if something happens to Henry. Guardians and successor trustees are named to act on behalf of the children if both parents should die. Probate is avoided, estate taxes are minimized, and the proper structure is in place to provide for the survivors.

Bank and Brokerage Accounts

If Henry had liquid savings in a bank or brokerage account, we would add a third LLC as the owner of the account. The ownership of the LLC would be placed in the trust. As we discussed, when our goal is privacy and asset protection we attach an asset protection vehicle—such as an LLC to the plan.

All financial accounts require the name and identifying information for the authorized signatory. Although the account is in the name of the LLC, we will need to provide a signatory. If Henry uses his name and Social Security number, the account will be disclosed in a search. The proper strategy is to have the trust company act as signatory. Henry can manage the investments and even make trades in the brokerage account. The trust company issues checks according to Henry's instructions.

With the Privacy Trust–Plan #2, the account is both private and protected. The account is in the LLC and Henry is not connected to it in the public filings or on the signature card. His ownership of the account won't be discovered through any available search techniques. If a lawsuit or a claim develops against Henry for any reason, the funds are legally insulated against liens or collection actions in the LLC.

Summary

Information about your financial life is a valuable commodity. With limited exceptions, public and private entities that have information about you use it to market products or sell it to others who do the marketing. County and state governments sell real estate ownership data, driving records, and court filings to list vendors and information brokers. Financial firms use sophisticated software to analyze your saving and spending patterns and target investment products you are likely to buy.

As a result, information about your real estate ownership is directly available for public view and financial accounts are immediately accessible by hundreds or hundreds of thousands of company employees and hired sales forces. From there, it is only a small step into the hands of a lawyer, business competitor, or a determined ex-spouse—armed and eager to use this information for personal advantage.

Since we cannot control the flow of personal information from the bank or brokerage firm, our approach is to restrict access in the first instance. If your name or identification number is on the record, you have provided valuable information about yourself that is subject to widespread dissemination. Instead, we recommend that you limit access to your ownership records and details by using a Privacy Trust to hold property and financial accounts.

A Privacy Trust can be created solely for the legitimate purpose of concealing the ownership of assets from public view in order to avoid privacy intrusions. This is often an important part of a sound plan for both business and personal reasons. The Privacy Trust–Plan #1 is designed to directly own your home and savings accounts, and to provide a convenient and cost effective strategy to accomplish privacy goals.

The Privacy Trust–Plan #2 is designed to add particular asset protection features to the overall plan. Property may be owned by an asset protection vehicle such as a corporation, Family Limited Partnership, or Limited Liability Company to shield Dangerous Assets from each other and from Safe Assets. The ownership of the entity is then held by the Privacy Trust.

In chapters 10, 11, and 12, we will discuss how advanced strategies, including domestic and offshore techniques can be added to the basic plan.

CHAPTER TEN

Adding the Safety Valve to Your Plan

A VARIETY OF SOPHISTICATED FEATURES can be added to the strategies we have discussed by taking advantage of laws designed to encourage privacy and asset protection goals. In this chapter, we will discuss a popular planning option known as the Asset Protection Trust and show you the opportunities for enhancing the structure of your overall plan.

The Asset Protection Trust

A popular and successful strategy for protecting privacy and assets is known as the Asset Protection Trust (APT). A recent report by the U.S. Department of the Treasury stated that in response to concerns about litigation the market for APTs is "exploding." The Treasury Department estimates that assets worth "tens of billions of dollars" are currently in these types of trusts with the number and amount growing rapidly each year. An article in the January

1996 *American Bar Association Journal* stated, ironically, that lawyers are seeking protection from the hazards of their profession by setting up APTs for themselves. As one attorney quoted in the article put it, *"I don't want someone doing to me what I do to them all day in court."*

The reason for the popularity of this technique is that it acts as an ultimate safety valve—providing an additional layer of protection for plans designed to avoid privacy intrusions and frivolous "deep pocket" litigation. Many individuals, wary of the potential for abusive lawsuits and frustrated by widespread violations of personal privacy, view the APT as an important component of a sound financial plan.

Features of the APT

In many ways an Asset Protection Trust looks like a standard domestic trust. The settlor is the person who transfers the assets to the trust. The settlor may be one of the trustees, together with a trust company, whose business is operated outside of the United States. The arrangement differs from Privacy Trust–Plan #1 and Privacy Trust–Plan #2 because, in this case, the trust company is located in a foreign country—outside the jurisdiction of U.S. courts. The Privacy Trust–Plan #3 takes advantage of favorable privacy and asset protection laws which exist in other parts of the world.

In a typical trust, the trustees are given discretion to accumulate or distribute income among a specified class of beneficiaries. The settlor may be one of the named beneficiaries, together with his spouse, children, or grandchildren. One unique feature of this kind of a trust is the role of the *Protector*. The Protector is a person, often the settlor, whose consent is necessary for certain activity by the trustees. The term of the trust may be limited to a period of years, or it may continue after the settlor's death.

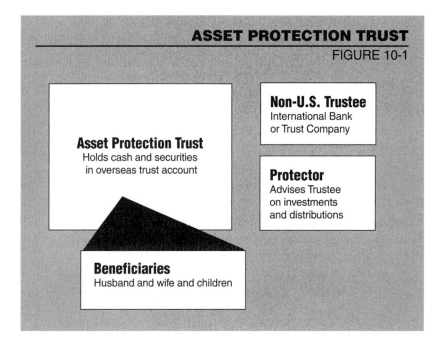

ASSET PROTECTION TRUST

FIGURE 10-1

Asset Protection Trust
Holds cash and securities
in overseas trust account

Non-U.S. Trustee
International Bank
or Trust Company

Protector
Advises Trustee
on investments
and distributions

Beneficiaries
Husband and wife and children

Moving Property Overseas

One way to use an APT is to transfer cash, securities, or other liquid assets to an account established under the name of the trust at a bank of your choice in a foreign jurisdiction. The Protector then advises the trustees on the manner in which the funds are to be held or invested. Income can be distributed to the beneficiaries or accumulated in the trust.

This arrangement, as shown in figure 10-1, provides excellent privacy and asset protection. As we will discuss, assets held in an overseas trust account—in a country with strict bank secrecy laws—can be a legitimate and powerful legal strategy.

Keeping Property in the U.S.

For those who want the option to transfer funds into an overseas account—but are reluctant to do so immediately, an alternative

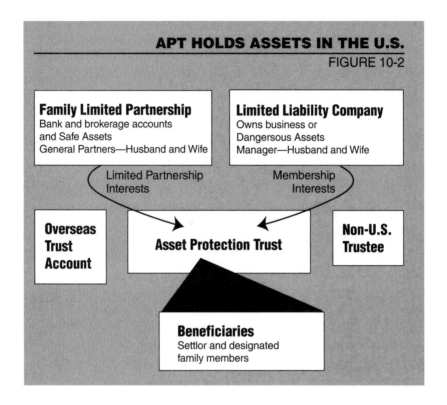

APT HOLDS ASSETS IN THE U.S.

FIGURE 10-2

Family Limited Partnership
Bank and brokerage accounts
and Safe Assets
General Partners—Husband and Wife

Limited Liability Company
Owns business or
Dangersous Assets
Manager—Husband and Wife

Limited Partnership
Interests

Membership
Interests

**Overseas
Trust
Account**

Asset Protection Trust

**Non-U.S.
Trustee**

Beneficiaries
Settlor and designated
family members

format is to use a domestic entity to maintain property in the United States. One method for accomplishing this is to use the Family Limited Partnership or Limited Liability Company in conjunction with the Asset Protection Trust. This popular strategy is illustrated in figure 10-2.

Under this arrangement, husband and wife are the general partners or members with complete management and control over the company. Only the membership or partnership interests are transferred to the trust. The strategy is similar to Privacy Trust–Plan #2—but the trust uses a foreign rather than a domestic trust company.

The trustee has no right to interfere in the management of the assets of the partnership or the LLC. Control is maintained by husband and wife as general partners or managers. Even though the trust holds the ownership interests, all of the assets remain physically located in the United States under the direct control and supervision of husband and wife.

This arrangement can provide a high level of asset protection benefits. Property is legally insulated within the FLP or LLC. The Asset Protection Trust owns and protects the *interests* in those entities. Liquid assets can be moved into the overseas trust account for additional protection or investment purposes.

■ Privacy Limitations

From a privacy standpoint, we know that funds transferred to the overseas trust account benefit from the local bank secrecy laws. But, under this arrangement, there are practical problems with creating privacy for domestic entities. If you are the signatory on the accounts and the real estate in the name of the FLP or LLC, your name and Social Security number will connect you to the property. As general partner of the FLP, your signature will be required for any legal activity of the FLP. If we make the offshore trustee the signatory on the bank accounts and the real estate, it will be inconvenient and time consuming to have the trustee transfer funds and execute legal documents as necessary.

Privacy Trust–Plan #3

We can overcome these practical difficulties and maximize privacy features, by combining our standard privacy strategy with the Asset Protection Trust. For convenience we describe this as the Privacy Trust–Plan #3. Here's how the parts of the plan fit together.

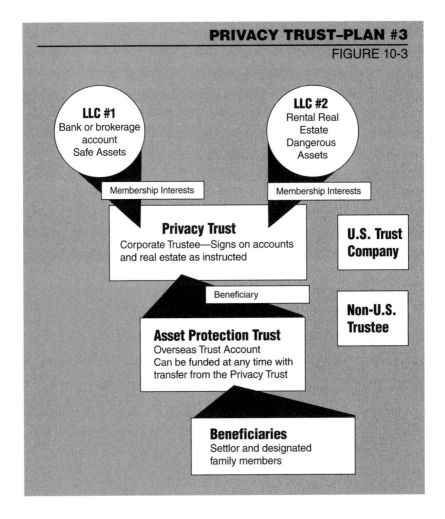

PRIVACY TRUST–PLAN #3

FIGURE 10-3

LLC #1
Bank or brokerage
account
Safe Assets

LLC #2
Rental Real
Estate
Dangerous
Assets

Membership Interests

Membership Interests

Privacy Trust
Corporate Trustee—Signs on accounts
and real estate as instructed

**U.S. Trust
Company**

Beneficiary

**Non-U.S.
Trustee**

Asset Protection Trust
Overseas Trust Account
Can be funded at any time with
transfer from the Privacy Trust

Beneficiaries
Settlor and designated
family members

1. We follow our asset protection principles by legally separating Dangerous and Safe Assets. Bank and brokerage accounts are insulated from liability associated with the real estate. Property is maintained domestically—nothing is moved offshore—protected by the LLCs. An LLC provides the same asset protection advantages as the FLP—but with greater privacy benefits. Since the FLP requires the signature of a general partner for legal action, privacy for the general partner involves more planning.

Our objectives at this point can be satisfied most directly with the LLC.

2. The Privacy Trust is the owner of the LLCs. The corporate trustee can act as signatory on accounts and execute real estate deeds and other documents according to the instructions you present—successfully concealing ownership of all property in the LLCs. At this point, the format is identical to the Privacy Trust–Plan #2.

3. For those who want the extra advantage and safety features available from an offshore trust, in Plan #3 we have designated the Asset Protection Trust as the beneficiary of the Privacy Trust. This creates the capability of moving funds into the overseas account at a later date for additional privacy, asset protection, or investment opportunities.

Advantages of the Asset Protection Trust

The Asset Protection Trust is a trust established under the laws of a country which are more favorable to privacy and asset protection objectives than the laws in the United States. For example, the laws in some countries provide for a statute of limitations on fraudulent conveyances which can be as short as one year and the standard of proof required for a fraudulent conveyance is the difficult "beyond a reasonable doubt" rather than the lesser civil standard of a "preponderance of the evidence." The courts in these countries will not enforce a judgment rendered in the United States, or an order of a U.S. Bankruptcy Court. To prosecute a claim against the trust, the creditor would have to go to that country and retry the underlying case, an almost impossible requirement.

A further advantage of the Asset Protection Trust is that a greater degree of flexibility can be achieved in the way in which the trust is established. The settlor of the trust can serve as both trustee and beneficiary, and the trust will still be valid under local law. This allows the settlor to retain a substantially greater degree of control and enjoyment over trust assets than would be permitted under U.S. law with a domestic trust.

Of equal importance, an Asset Protection Trust allows a great deal of practical flexibility because the option is always available to move the assets into an account established in the foreign jurisdiction—subject to the protective features of local law. To reach those funds, the creditor would have to commence an action in the foreign jurisdiction and would have to overcome significant obstacles under the law of that jurisdiction.

The problem for a creditor with a judgment is that a U.S. court has no capacity to exercise its authority over a foreign trustee. Simply stated, a foreign person or company with no presence or assets in the United States cannot be compelled to act by a U.S. court. If a U.S. court ordered a foreign trustee to return assets, the foreign trustee, under a duty to preserve trust property, would refuse to comply with the order.

If a foreign person or entity has assets in the United States, a court can exercise leverage by threatening or attempting to seize those assets for failure to comply with the order of the court. For example, on occasion the U.S. Government seeks information about foreign bank deposits in matters concerning criminal tax evasion, drug charges, or securities law violations. Because of its local secrecy laws, the foreign bank usually fails to comply with the government's request for information. However, when the foreign bank has assets, such as deposits or branches in the United States, the government may threaten to seize the assets if the bank does not comply with the court order. Generally, this threat is successful and the bank will reveal the sought-after information.

Precisely for this reason, most foreign based trust companies do not conduct business or have assets in the United States. Any foreign trustee which is selected must have no local business activity in order to avoid the financial leverage which might then be applied by a U.S. court.

Since the creditor cannot obtain satisfaction by obtaining a U.S. court order against a foreign trustee, the only method for compelling the trustee to act is to file a lawsuit in the jurisdiction in which the trustee is located. Whether or not the creditor can be successful in this forum will depend upon the particular laws in effect in that country.

Contempt Orders Against U.S. Debtor

Can you, a U.S. resident and a settlor of the Asset Protection Trust, be ordered by a court to return assets transferred to the offshore account? A judgment creditor would certainly like to obtain such an order from the local court and whether he can do so depends upon the terms of the trust.

Clearly, if you have the right to retrieve the assets, a judge will order you to do so. Judges back up these orders with the power to hold a person in *contempt of court* for refusing to comply. The sole issue then is your legal ability to return transferred property pursuant to a court order.

This issue is resolved, in a properly drafted trust, by not giving the settlor any such power to revoke the trust or reacquire the assets without the consent of the trustee. Although the trustee typically will comply with the wishes of the settlor, the trust agreement requires the trustee to disregard any communications issued by the settlor under *duress*. That is, if the settlor is ordered by a court to communicate with the trustee, the trustee is required by the terms of the trust to ignore such requests for action.

As a result of this structure, the settlor has no legal right to revoke the trust and reacquire trust assets. A court cannot compel an action that an individual has no power to perform, and the foreign trustee will not respond to orders from a court outside of its jurisdiction. The conclusion is that the assets of the trust are protected, and the settlor should not be in contempt for failing to achieve a return of the property.

The result may be different when the Asset Protection Trust is used as a scheme to defraud creditors or the IRS, or to protect the proceeds of criminal or fraudulent activities. In these cases, where the defendant is perceived as a "bad guy," the judge may ignore the provisions of the trust document and apply the leverage of a civil contempt order. The APT is not designed to allow individuals to defraud others or engage in tax evasion or criminal conduct. If the trust is used for an illegitimate purpose, significant legal pressure—including contempt sanctions—may be brought to bear on the offender.

Where to Create the Asset Protection Trust

Selecting the proper jurisdiction for the Asset Protection Trust is a matter of critical importance. As a general rule, the jurisdiction should have a well-established trust law favorable to asset protection strategies. Further, it should be inconvenient or nearly impossible for a U. S. creditor to reach the assets of the trust by commencing an action in the foreign country.

Key Factors

Consider the following factors when selecting a jurisdiction for an APT:

Ease of Communications

Communication with the foreign trustee must be convenient. Fortunately, the use of e-mail and fax as well as improvements in telephone technology have made communication with even the most geographically remote locations a relatively simple procedure. Using only English speaking countries avoids language barriers which can cause delays or costly mistakes.

Experienced and Well-Established Trustees

The country where the trust is established must provide a choice of responsible and experienced trust companies from which to select a trustee. The trust companies must be experienced in the area of asset protection and understand the nature of their peculiar responsibilities.

No or Low Tax Jurisdiction

Income earned by the Asset Protection Trust must not be subject to taxation in that jurisdiction.

Strict Bank Secrecy Laws

The country must prohibit disclosure of customer information by local trust companies and financial institutions.

Favorable Trust Laws

Many foreign jurisdictions do not recognize the existence of trusts or severely restrict these arrangements. It is important that the law of the country allows the greatest degree of flexibility in establishing the trust to meet privacy and asset protection objectives.

Stable Local Government

Political and economic stability is essential to the proper functioning of the trust. A country which may have its legal system or its financial institutions disrupted by unexpected forces should not be chosen.

Favorable Asset Protection Laws

The existence of laws designed to encourage the formation of trusts used for asset protection strategies is an essential factor. If a creditor elects to file a lawsuit in the foreign jurisdiction seeking to set aside the trust, the laws of that country must make it impractical for the creditor to obtain a successful result. A country which has no treaties with the U.S. and does not enforce foreign judgments is critical to the success of the plan.

Absence of Exchange or Currency Controls

The ability to move funds, if necessary, in and out of the jurisdiction without interference or restriction by local authorities is a requirement in selecting a location.

Confidentiality

The country which is chosen must allow for complete confidentiality of information concerning the settlor and the beneficiaries of the trust.

The Most Favorable Laws

Countries that have some or all of the features mentioned above include the Bahamas, Bermuda, the Cayman Islands, the Cook Islands, and Gibraltar.

The Bahamas

The Bahamas is one of the oldest and most established financial centers in the world. It has strict bank secrecy laws, no income tax, and a modern and sophisticated telecommunications structure. The location in the Caribbean is convenient to the United States. There are a number of excellent trust companies located in the Bahamas, and local law allows a satisfactory degree of flexibility in the creation of Asset Protection Trusts.

Bermuda

Bermuda is a group of English speaking islands located in the western Atlantic Ocean approximately 800 miles from New York City. Bermuda has a well-developed modern trust law. The country has no income tax or other form of taxation for profits or capital gains. Some professional advisers have complained that the Bermuda trust companies are difficult to work with, but it is hard to say whether these are isolated incidents or whether it represents a pattern of conduct sufficient to cause one to avoid Bermuda for these types of purposes.

The Cayman Islands

The Cayman Islands are a group of three islands conveniently located just one hour's flight from Miami. The main island is Grand Cayman, which has developed into a major offshore financial center. The population is small and homogeneous and enjoys a high standard of living. The islands also enjoy an exceptional degree of political and economic stability. The trust law of the Cayman Islands provides excellent asset protection features, and numerous trust companies are experienced and well-established. The Cayman Islands have strict bank secrecy provisions and no local income taxes. The islands are one of the most popular places for establishing Asset Protection Trusts.

The Cook Islands

The Cook Islands was the first jurisdiction to enact legislation encouraging the formation of Asset Protection Trusts. All trust companies are licensed and regulated by the government of the Cook Islands with the strictest qualification and capitalization standards.

The Cook Islands is located in the South Pacific near Tahiti and Samoa. Until 1965, the country was a protectorate of New Zealand and is now self-governed with its own legislature and prime minister. Communication facilities are excellent with modern international telephone, telex, and facsimile services via satellite. The Cook Islands are in the same time zone as Hawaii—two hours behind Pacific Standard Time and five hours behind Eastern Standard Time.

Since the enactment of the International Trusts Amendment Act of 1989, the Cook Islands have been the jurisdiction of choice for the creation of Asset Protection Trusts. The law provides the highest degree of protection, flexibility, and privacy. The trust companies in the Cook Islands are experienced and knowledgeable with an unblemished record of competency, thoroughness, and integrity unmatched by any other country in the world.

Gibraltar

Gibraltar is a British territory located off the coast of Spain at the western entrance to the Mediterranean. It is well-known as a convenient international offshore haven and has many local professionals and trust companies of high quality and reputation. Foreign trusts are not subject to any taxes in Gibraltar. The trust laws contain some favorable asset protection features. Asset Protection Trusts established in Gibraltar by Amendments to the Bankruptcy Ordinance are registered with the local government. Although access to this special register is limited to the local government, some practitioners are concerned that confidentiality may be impaired by this requirement.

Using the APT to Avoid Taxes

It is difficult to imagine an issue that is so clear yet produces as much confusion as the proper U.S. tax treatment of the Asset Protection Trust. Despite thousands of Web sites on the Internet promoting offshore trusts as legitimate strategies for avoiding income taxes—this is not the case. The APT does not provide any income tax advantage. *All of the income of the trust is included on the tax return of the U.S. settlor of the trust.* The trust is treated in the same manner as a revocable living trust. This rule applies whether the assets of the trust are located in the U.S. or in an overseas account. It also applies regardless of whether the source of the income is from the U.S. or from another country. All income of the trust is taxable on the return of the settlor in the year it is earned. It doesn't matter when the funds are distributed or returned to the U.S. *There is no strategy or technique which will alter this result without causing you to commit perjury or tax fraud.*

This treatment is beneficial from an asset protection standpoint because it allows us to transfer property to and from an APT without creating any tax consequences. No gain or loss is recognized, and no taxable income is produced by a contribution or distribution.

Depending on the way the trust is structured, there may be certain disclosure requirements provided by law. The Small Business Investment Act of 1996 created specified filing requirements for trusts which meet the definition of a "Foreign Trust." However, most APTs can be structured so that no additional reporting is necessary. We will discuss this issue in greater detail later in chapter 13.

Summary

You can take advantage of favorable laws in other countries to enhance the privacy and asset protection features of any plan.

One technique is to deposit funds in an overseas account in the name of an Asset Protection Trust. Investments are managed by the trust company with advice and direction from the Protector. This strategy can create excellent financial privacy when the overseas account is located in a country with strict bank secrecy and confidentiality laws.

Individuals who do not wish to transfer property overseas—until it is necessary to do so—prefer to use the Asset Protection Trust as a safety valve. Property and liquid assets are held in domestic entities such as an LLC or FLP. At a later point, if additional protection is required, assets can be transferred to the overseas trust account to be held according to the terms of the trust agreement.

For those seeking financial privacy for assets held in the U.S., such as real estate and bank accounts, we have suggested the Privacy Trust–Plan #3. Under this arrangement, property and accounts are held by one or more LLCs. These companies are owned by a Privacy Trust with a U.S. trust company acting as the signatory for the companies. This plan effectively conceals ownership of financial accounts, real estate, and business interests. The Asset Protection Trust is added to the plan as a beneficiary of the Privacy Trust—again, to act as a safety valve to maximize the overall protection.

CHAPTER ELEVEN

The Role of Privacy Havens

W E HAVE SEEN THAT FINANCIAL PRIVACY is an increasingly scarce and valuable commodity. Privacy is desirable because it minimizes particular dangers which we face. In the United States, these dangers are often the product of a lawsuit system which unfairly targets those with property or savings. In all other countries—with fewer lawyers and lawsuits—the threat of litigation is not the primary concern. Instead, privacy issues are related to the political and economic climate which pose risks with varying degrees of severity.

Political Threats

In many countries the greatest dangers to wealth may arise in the political arena. A friendly government can be voted out or overthrown, or the existing government may radically alter its political course. Recently, the opposition candidates were elected president of South Korea and mayor of Mexico City. Whenever the party in power changes, there is a massive redistribution of wealth as business ties with supporters of the old regime are cut and new relationships with new supporters are forged.

In every country, to greater or lesser degrees, the success of a business depends upon the relationship with the proper government officials. Contracts, licenses, permits, and privileges are granted to those who are able to cultivate influence at the right levels of government. When power in the government shifts from one faction to another, there can be a dramatic reshuffling of the wealth in society. Money and influence shift to the friends of the newly empowered, and those previously excluded enjoy their day in the sun.

The political and business forces removed from power face varying degrees of retribution. Cuba's Fidel Castro confiscated the property of the Battista supporters and thousands were jailed. Business associates of the Shah of Iran were forced to flee the country, leaving behind their homes and savings. In the U.S., political ideology is secondary to an uninterrupted flow of campaign contributions. A change of administration only impacts those business owners who foolishly bet everything on the losing candidate and are unable to make amends with the winner.

Fiscal Crises

Wealth also can be attacked by ill-conceived political and fiscal policies, which weaken the local currency and devalue the accumulated wealth of the population. In Indonesia, Thailand, and South Korea, as a result of entrenched corruption and a badly mismanaged economic system, the value of the currency has recently declined up to 80 percent. The cumulative savings of much of the citizenry have been obliterated. Strict exchange controls, forbidding the movement of assets out of the country or into a stronger currency, has disproportionately penalized that portion of the population without sufficient resources or ingenuity to successfully avoid these laws.

Political instability, potential devaluation of the currency, and the threat of exchange controls pose dangers to individuals in almost every country around the world at one time or another. At this moment, the Asian economies are in turmoil—prompting severe political and social change. Not long ago, these countries were among the strongest in the world. In the United States, the massive inflation of the 1970s and early 1980s resulted in wage and price controls, limited exchange controls, 20 percent interest rates, and a critically devalued dollar. The Russian ruble has become nearly worthless since the collapse of the Soviet Union. The German mark has suffered under the weight of the obligations created by the unification of East and West Germany. In Indonesia, millions of ethnic Chinese, long the most prosperous group in the country, are preparing to flee to avoid the violence and scapegoating which inevitably follow an economic collapse.

To protect against the financial consequences of a shift of political power and to avoid controls on the flow of funds, those who have accumulated wealth rely on financial privacy to ensure their livelihood and their physical safety. The universal strategy for those who can afford to do so is to keep what they own well hidden—outside the country—in a jurisdiction that specializes in providing privacy services.

Understanding Financial Privacy Havens

Many countries outside the United States recognize and appreciate financial privacy as a traditional and important right of their citizens. The European nations impose a variety of safeguards to limit unauthorized disclosure of personal information. The members of the European Union have imposed strict controls over the dissemination of personal data. Companies are not permitted to gather personal information or use it for marketing purposes without an individual's consent. This law effectively bars the type of cross-selling and information peddling engaged in by U.S. companies.

Germany has particularly stringent laws governing the use of personal data. For example, in return for the right to market its credit cards in Germany, Citigroup agreed to allow German inspectors to regularly monitor its giant computer databases—located in South Dakota—to ensure that Germany's privacy laws are not violated. The European countries are acutely sensitive to the issue—having witnessed firsthand the consequences of privacy abuses from the Nazi and communist regimes.

Elsewhere in the world, out of purely practical concerns, countries have recognized that meeting the demand for financial privacy can be a lucrative source of business. These countries are generally referred to as financial privacy havens or tax havens or off-shore havens.

Often, the privacy havens have limited domestic resources. Sometimes they are geographically isolated with limited opportunity for economic expansion. Especially for the Caribbean nations, the clean, well-paying jobs and steady revenue source provided by a financial services industry can be an attractive complement or alternative to a complete reliance on tourist dollars.

Competition to Attract Business

Like all businesses with attractive profit opportunities, tax havens must compete with each other to attract a volume of banking and financial services clients. This was not always the case. Only twenty years ago a few well-known centers such as the Bahamas, Bermuda, the Cayman Islands, and Switzerland were the predominant service providers in this area.

Within the last ten years, many new countries have developed the necessary package of banking services and asset protection products. There are now a significant number of countries seeking this business, and competition is fierce. Successful countries attract this business with some or all of the traditional techniques: better service, innovative products, favorable laws and regulations, and competitive prices. When a particular country develops a financial product that satisfies a wide demand, it may leapfrog over its competitors to the top ranks of the financial centers.

■ Asset Protection and the Cook Islands

For example, the Cook Islands was a quiet tourist destination in the South Pacific. In an effort to diversify the economy, the legislature enacted laws to develop a competitive tax haven– and financial services business. In 1989, Cook Islands officials recognized the explosive growth potential for asset protection services and developed the first comprehensive legislation to allow the formation of Asset Protection Trusts. The new law eliminated the ambiguities and difficulties which existed with these trusts in other parts of the world and established convenient and flexible rules allowing individuals to accomplish their privacy and asset protection objectives from a single source.

As expected, the market for the asset protection services grew rapidly, largely in response to the unchecked litigation frenzy and what many perceive as increased government and commercial encroachment on individual privacy rights. As the premier provider of these services, the Cook Islands quickly established itself as a leader in financial services and attracted much of the worldwide total business in the field.

The popularity of asset protection and the revenue and capital attracted to the Cook Islands has not gone unnoticed by the other tax havens. Over the last few years, many of the old line financial centers have passed asset protection legislation or have focused on developing the expertise to attract asset protection business. We receive calls each month from government officials and bankers in the tax haven jurisdictions inquiring about the best way to develop a strong asset protection business. New entries include, for example, the nations of Nevis, Belize, Antigua, and Turks and Caicos—each of which is actively promoting its asset protection services.

The generally healthy competition between countries for this business has produced a vast array of creative financial, investment, privacy, and asset protection products. These techniques can be used in combination with a variety of legal entities to produce powerful legal protection. Wealthy American individuals, who can afford the highest priced legal talent, shield their property with elaborate strategies designed by experienced international tax attorneys. The purpose is to blend the right financial product with the proper legal structure to produce a successful result— with the highest degree of financial privacy and asset protection. We will discuss the products which are available and the structures which accommodate these products. First, let's examine the common characteristics of the financial privacy havens to see why they attract so much of the money in the world.

The Tax Haven Money Magnets

We are all familiar or have at least heard about financial centers such as the Bahamas, Hong Kong, Singapore, Liechtenstein, the Cayman Islands, and Monaco. Fewer know that Tonga, Nauru, Maldives, Guam, and Nevis are also popular tax havens.

The common characteristics in the offshore havens are:

■ A system of low or no taxes.

■ Maximum flexibility and secrecy in the ownership of business entities.

■ Strict bank secrecy rules.

This powerful package of services is in high demand from individuals throughout the world seeking privacy for their wealth and protection of assets from government or economic instability. And let's not forget about taxes. There is a massive flow of funds from the high tax countries—the United States, Canada, and Europe—into the tax havens.

For example, studies show that when tax rates in a country move above 30 percent, to the 40 percent and higher range, tax avoidance becomes a preoccupation of many individuals and businesses. Much of Europe, the United States, and Canada have progressive tax rates which approach or exceed 50 percent—providing an endless source of demand for the attractive services offered by the tax havens.

A recent study showed that 50 percent of all international transactions are directed through the tax haven jurisdictions. Hundreds of billions of dollars in international trade and commerce are routed through these countries each day. These nations allow the greatest degree of freedom in the ownership and operation of a business, and there is little government interference with business activities. It is only natural that international buying and selling of products and services, whenever feasible, are routed to a jurisdiction that protects the privacy of the parties and provides little or no taxation.

Common Tax Strategies

Goods which are imported into the U.S. are often routed or invoiced through a company established in one of the tax havens. Products exported from the U.S. may be "sold" first to a tax haven company to drop most of the profit in the no tax jurisdiction. This technique is known as *offsite pricing*, and the goal is to move profits from a high tax country to a low or no tax country.

Let's say that you are in the business of importing cheese from Holland. Each year you buy $100,000 worth of cheese which you sell for $200,000 to local supermarkets. That's a gross profit of $100,000 before other expenses, and that income is subject to tax in the U.S. at the normal rates.

What if you could work it differently? Instead of buying from Holland directly, you set up a company in the Bahamas to buy the cheese. That company then sells the cheese to you in America for $150,000. Now, when you sell to grocery stores, your gross profit is only $50,000 not $100,000. The other $50,000 in profit was earned by the Bahamas company where there is no income tax.

Companies that export goods often use the same basic strategy. A U.S. company sells T-shirts to France for $3 per shirt. It sells 100,000 shirts per year for a gross of $300,000. Instead of shipping directly, the orders come from a company in Hong Kong at a price of $1.50 per shirt. The Hong Kong company now sells the shirts to France for the full $3. As a result of this arrangement, the U.S. company now has gross income of only $150,000. The balance was earned in Hong Kong, where there is no tax on this income.

Despite provisions in the tax law and regulations which prohibit or restrict the use of these strategies, the demand from citizens of high tax countries for these techniques is powerful. Those who receive royalty income from patents or copyrights such as book authors, software developers, and inventors often transfer these rights to offshore companies and have the funds collected in a tax haven jurisdiction. Owners of appreciating stock, which includes almost every man, woman, and child in the Silicon Valley, seek to move and sell the asset in a country that does not tax this income. Founders and employees of successful companies may receive stock options representing a substantial portion of their wealth. Avoiding the tax on the gain is always an important consideration. Individuals with large investment portfolios or those who want to avoid a large tax bite on their investment earnings are eager to shift to non-tax jurisdictions.

Fighting the Lure of the Tax Havens

Naturally enough the high tax countries are not happy to see resources and tax money flow out of the country. There are huge government bureaucracies to maintain, expensive new weapon systems to be developed, and social programs to be financed. The top priority of every government is generating funds to carry out its policies. Every high tax country, with greater or lesser degrees of success, attempts to thwart the powerful and seductive appeal of the tax havens.

At least for now, the tax havens appear to be winning the war for the hearts and the wallets of the citizens of the world. The difficulty faced by the high tax forces is that it is impossible to physically block the flow of funds from one country to another. Money moves electronically, at the speed of light, from bank to bank. Every hour of every day trillions of dollars and francs and yen are shifted instantaneously between banks in every part of the world. Governments themselves use these electronic transfer systems to make purchases, pay debts, and settle accounts between each other. Shutting down this free flow of money around the world would seriously impair international commerce and economic life as it exists today.

The best that the high tax country can do is attempt to gather information from within its banking system about capital movements by individuals. This is not an easy task. On its face, a legitimate business transfer to an overseas account looks no different than a tax motivated transfer. For example, bank records in the home country may reveal that money was transferred from a domestic bank to a bank in Luxembourg. Whether this transaction was a normal business transaction or part of a scheme to avoid taxes cannot be determined from the record of the transaction itself.

More information is needed to determine the true character of the transfer. Officials in the home country can question the individual, but it is unlikely that this would be productive. What they would like to do is trace the money to see whether its uses are legitimate and whether the proper taxes are paid to the home country.

But now the tax haven country stands up to do its job. Officials in the home country will be denied access to information about the funds and their recipient. Secrecy laws prevent disclosure of account information by the recipient bank. Home country tax officials must attempt to develop their case without the cooperation of the tax haven authorities. Sometimes the funds are moved rapidly through a series of banks in different jurisdictions, but this is only necessary when there is some doubt about security at the initial recipient bank.

Nations can and do make treaties with each other to exchange information, assist each other in law enforcement, and provide for convenient tax administration. But these treaties are generally between high tax countries with similar economic interests. The United States has an extensive network of treaties with the western European countries allowing for a mutual enforcement of judg-

THE TAX COLLECTOR'S BATTLE FOR INFORMATION

The battle between tax authorities and beleaguered citizens sometimes reaches nearly comic proportions. In 1983, French tax authorities announced that they had broken into the computerized records of Union Bank of Switzerland and obtained the names of 5,000 French citizens with accounts at the bank. Having such accounts was a violation of French exchange control laws at the time. The French Government offered leniency if the guilty parties would voluntarily come forward. Union Bank of Switzerland vehemently denied that such a list even existed because its account holders are not referenced by nationality. After much blustering and posturing it was determined that, indeed, the French were bluffing—the list was a fabrication—and two customs agents who attempted to follow a French citizen across the Swiss border were arrested by Swiss authorities and spent several months in jail.

ments, minimal trade restrictions, and a comprehensive tax program for international transactions. The high tax countries have a mutual interest in cooperating with each other.

Tax haven countries, as a rule, do not enter into treaties which would impact their special services. The greater the level of cooperation with the high tax countries, the greater the impairment of its usefulness as a tax secrecy haven. Even when there is agreement for some form of mutual assistance, disclosure of information is limited to severe and enumerated criminal offenses. Tax violations are not included in this category.

The high tax countries are frustrated by their inability to restrict the natural flow of currency and tax dollars from high to low tax jurisdictions. This frustration inevitably leads to greater restrictions on freedom and privacy. Governments always want more disclosure and more reports about financial transactions to bolster their investigative powers. Sometimes the information which the government seeks is intended to protect legitimate interests in tax revenue and currency value. But too often, throughout history, we have seen that the government's purpose in gathering information is to increase political power, carry out surveillance of political enemies, suppress dissent, or conduct any number of abusive activities against its citizens.

Governments want information about their citizens, and citizens want privacy and protection from the exercise of any government authority which threatens their financial security and accumulated wealth. The offshore havens satisfy the demand for financial privacy and security with a powerful arsenal of products designed to accomplish these specific results. In the next chapter, we will discuss the privacy and protection strategies which are available.

CHAPTER TWELVE

Offshore Privacy Strategies

THE OFFSHORE HAVENS offer an elaborate variety of products and services that can be arranged to create sophisticated and imaginative privacy and asset protection strategies.

Bank Secrecy

The cornerstone product offered by every offshore haven is a legal system that protects against unwanted and unauthorized disclosure of financial matters. Bank secrecy means that, by law, bank employees are prohibited from revealing information concerning a customer's account. This prohibition is buttressed by criminal sanctions including fines and imprisonment.

The mutual goal of the financial institution and the government in the offshore jurisdiction is to protect the confidentiality of the customer's business matters from third party inquiries. Foreign governments, creditors, spouses, and litigants cannot legally obtain information concerning the existence or activity of any account.

An early expression of the importance of bank secrecy laws were regulations formulated by Frederick the Great in 1765.

"We forbid on pain of royal displeasure anyone from investigating the banking assets of anyone else. Nor shall bank employees disclose such information to third parties, whether verbally or in writing, on pain of dismissal and criminal prosecution. They must, on accepting employment, solemnly swear that any transactions that come to their attention in the course of their work will be considered the greatest secret that will be carried with them into the grave."

But as we have seen, with few exceptions, these principles of individual financial privacy in the Western democracies have yielded to the power of commercial interests, tax authorities, and litigants in a broad variety of civil matters. Most often, the bank acts on its own behalf to gather and distribute customer account information for marketing purposes.

Increasingly, the banks assume the role of agents for the government, collecting and feeding information on customers directly to the tax authorities. In Sweden, tax collectors have virtually unlimited access to all personal and financial information of account holders. French and British authorities have similar access, and banks must notify officials of the amount of interest earned on an account.

U.S. law requires that financial institutions provide the government with the names and Social Security numbers of account holders. The earnings on every account must be submitted, and copies of every transaction must be retained and made available to those with the proper legal authority.

A recently announced proposal by the Federal Deposit Insurance Corp. to "Know Your Customer" would require banks to set internal policies to verify customers' identities and sources of income. They would also have to monitor accounts for evidence of "suspicious transactions" that might indicate illegal activities or money laundering. Under this proposal, any larger than usual cash withdrawal or deposit would obligate the bank to inquire about the use or source of the funds. Unless the customer provides a satisfactory explanation, the bank is required to alert law enforcement authorities.

In marked contrast to the U.S. system which allows virtually unlimited collection, access, and marketing of personal financial data, the European Union now places severe restrictions on information collection and prohibits disclosure and commercial uses— without permission from the individual. Perhaps because of their firsthand experience with totalitarianism, the Europeans—more so than Americans— are acutely sensitive to the dangers of privacy intrusions and personal information gathering techniques from government or private agencies.

European countries which have preserved or developed a tradition of bank secrecy include Austria, Switzerland, Liechtenstein, Luxembourg, the Channel Islands, and Gibraltar. In the Caribbean the established havens are the Bahamas, Bermuda, and the Cayman Islands. Some of the newer entries such as the Cook Islands and Turks and Caicos now provide legitimate bank secrecy products.

It is advisable to be wary of those countries offering privacy services which have a significant level of political and social corruption. In certain countries, it is well-known among professionals, that for a modest bribe to the right person—a bank employee or government official—the purported secrecy would quickly evaporate. If there is any uncertainty on this issue it is probably best to choose other available alternatives.

Bank Secrecy Havens

Switzerland

Switzerland remains one of the most important banking centers in the world. It has a long history and tradition of financial privacy, which can be traced back to the Middle Ages. The Swiss Constitution, the Banking Law, and the Penal Code provide a solid legal foundation for maintaining the strict standards of confidentiality.

As a practical matter, Swiss banks and their employees do not disclose information except by direct judicial order. This practice applies to requests for information by individuals, foreign governments, the Swiss government, and to other banks. An employee who even acknowledges the existence of an account is in violation of the law.

Increasing Cooperation in Criminal Matters   In recent years, there has been a shift in the absolute secrecy policy in response to international pressures from the U.S. and other countries. In cases which involve requests for information from foreign governments concerning a serious criminal offense, the Swiss may cooperate in supplying the requested bank records. The foreign government must first show that a particular individual committed one of the enumerated crimes, which is also an offense in Switzerland. It must then present evidence that the individual has used an identified bank for transactions, which are associated with the crime. If the proof is determined to be satisfactory, the bank will be required to turn over records regarding the specific transactions involved. Account records not related to the transactions will not be disclosed.

Consistent with this new spirit of responsiveness but much to everyone's surprise the Swiss Government froze the accounts of exiled Philippine dictator Ferdinand Marcos and deposed Haiti ruler François "Papa Doc" Duvalier when the new governments began an effort to retrieve looted funds, which had been stashed in Switzerland. The official policy of the Swiss banks is now to refuse deposits from political leaders when the source of the funds appears to have been illegal or corrupt practices.

This increased cooperation regarding criminal matters has not been extended to civil cases. Disclosure of account information is still prohibited in all civil matters including divorce, lawsuits, and creditor claims. Swiss law also does not permit the disclosure of bank information to foreign tax authorities, including the Internal Revenue Service. Tax evasion is not a criminal offense in Switzerland and is not subject to the exclusion from secrecy of the specified crimes.

Advantages of Swiss Accounts   For reasons apart from bank secrecy, Switzerland provides a number of significant advantages. The banks provide the finest level of service available anywhere in the world. Bank personnel are justifiably famous for their knowledge and experience. The banks offer a broad range of services including securities brokerage and portfolio management. The location in the heart of Europe is convenient, the infrastructure and communication facilities are among the best in the world, and the political and social systems offer unparalleled stability.

Forms of Ownership   Swiss accounts are often held in the name of a corporation. The corporation can be formed in any part of the world and need not be a Swiss company. For example, it is not uncommon to form a corporation in the British Virgin Islands and to open an account for the company at a Swiss bank. These corporations may have bearer shares, which protect the true identity of the owner. We will discuss the uses of these types of corporations later.

Opening the Swiss account in the name of a trust is also an attractive option. Although Switzerland does not have its own laws for creating Asset Protection Trusts, an APT formed elsewhere can hold the account. A common approach is to form the trust under the laws of the Cook Islands with a Cook Islands trustee. The trust account is then opened in Switzerland to take advantage of the superior banking facilities.

Switzerland has joined in the cooperative spirit to discourage the use of secret accounts by those engaged in illegal activities. All Swiss banks are required to know the identity of their customers and the beneficial owner of an account. All account opening documentation must be accompanied by a Form A, which states the true name of the beneficial owner. This record is then maintained in a protected fashion with access restricted to the appropriate bank personnel.

Under limited circumstances, the disclosure of the beneficial owner required under Form A can be avoided. Under Swiss law, a Swiss attorney is permitted to open an account on behalf of an unnamed client. A declaration must be made on Form B that the disclosure would have serious legal ramifications for the client.

As we discuss the various structures involving companies and trusts which can be used to hold these accounts, we will see that the disclosure of the beneficial account owner on Form A or its equivalent actually increases the customer's protection by eliminating the issue of who is entitled to the funds.

Costs of Swiss Banking   The only significant drawback in Switzerland is that the cost of operating an account is comparatively high.

As always, excellent service and personal attention command a premium price in the market. Lately though, some of the smaller and medium-size banks have attempted to attract business from the three largest banks by pricing their services at a more reasonable level. As competition for business heats up, all of the banks will ultimately reduce their fees and a new class of customers will be developed.

Liechtenstein

Liechtenstein is a small country, neighboring Switzerland with a population of about 25,000 people. Its primary business is supplying the demand for financial secrecy through banking services and a variety of legal structures which allow maximum protection and anonymity in the ownership of property.

The Anstalt An entity which is unique to Liechtenstein is called an *Anstalt*, which is German for the word "establishment." The *Anstalt* combines the best features of a corporation with the flexibility of the trust. It can conduct a business, yet its owners are protected from personal liability. At the same time, the terms of the agreement can provide for distributions of income or principal according to the owners' wishes, just as in a trust. The *Anstalt* is managed by a board of directors, which can be a single individual.

USING AN *ANSTALT*

A short time ago we established an *Anstalt* for a client who made several million dollars when he sold his computer software company. He wanted to make sure that he preserved this money for his family's needs and his retirement. The sale proceeds were deposited in the *Anstalt*, which he then used to buy a new home in California and to make stock investments—all with complete anonymity and privacy.

The most popular feature is that the ownership of the *Anstalt* is completely secret. International corporations often use these arrangements to conceal stock ownership in other companies. Wealthy individuals anonymously acquire properties and companies with the privacy protection of the *Anstalt*. At the Senate Iran-Contra hearings, the CIA disclosed that it conducts much of its clandestine business activities through *Anstalts* in order to conceal its financial ownership in different companies.

The Stiftung   A second entity permitted under Liechtenstein law is known as the *Stiftung*. This more nearly resembles a trust or a foundation and is generally formed for the purpose of providing education and support for the members of the founder's family. The identity of the person creating the *Stiftung* may remain anonymous. Unlike the *Anstalt*, the law provides that a *Stiftung* is generally prohibited from engaging in any commercial business activity.

The *Anstalt* and the *Stiftung* can be used to own assets such as bank accounts or property in Liechtenstein or in any other country. Many Swiss bank accounts are owned in the name of an *Anstalt*, created to hold the accumulated wealth of an individual.

Liechtenstein provides complex legal structures and sophisticated banking services, which can be used by wealthy individuals and companies to accomplish an excellent level of asset protection and financial privacy.

Cayman Islands

The Cayman Islands is one of the largest and most popular financial centers. It provides a wide range of products and services that can be used to develop almost every conceivable tax and asset protection strategy.

The Caymans are located in the western Caribbean, convenient to the business centers in the U.S. More than 500 international banks have offices in the Caymans, including nearly every one of the top fifty in the world. More than 20,000 companies are registered in the country.

This activity and prosperity is due to four main factors:

1. There are no income taxes, capital gains taxes, profits tax, or estate taxes.

2. Bank secrecy laws are among the strictest in the world with criminal penalties for unauthorized disclosure.

3. The law allows companies to be formed with a minimum of paperwork. Shares can be held anonymously in bearer form or by nominees.

4. The law regarding the formation of trusts is highly developed and allows an excellent level of flexibility, asset protection, and privacy.

The Cayman Islands is what is known as a "booking center." That means that business transactions are routed through the Cayman Islands to take advantage of the favorable tax laws. An Italian shoe company, ultimately selling to a U.S. department store, might sell first to a Cayman subsidiary. That company then sells to the U.S. company. The effect is to "book" the sale in the Caymans— with a zero tax rate— rather than in Italy with its high corporate tax.

Wealthy individuals immigrating to the United States, generally stop off in a tax haven such as the Cayman Islands. U.S. residents and citizens pay income tax on their worldwide income and estate tax on all property, wherever located. Before settling in America and becoming subject to its tax laws, an individual will strip himself of his ownership rights. This is accomplished with corporations or trusts which allow the advantages of control and enjoyment of the assets without the disadvantages of high income and estate taxes.

Bank Secrecy Products

Let's look now at the bank secrecy and associated products which are offered by the tax havens.

To define the nature of the services which are offered, it is important to understand the nature of bank secrecy. Whom are we keeping the secrets from? Who should have access to information about the account?

The basic requirement of bank secrecy is that account information—the name of the depositor and account transactions—must not be disclosed to third parties. Third parties include both external sources such as foreign governments and internal sources such as the domestic government. Bank policy and law must provide that no information concerning any account may be disclosed to any person other than the customer.

Some customers desire an additional level of privacy—wishing to remain anonymous from all bank employees except the one or two managers of the branch. For example, a well-known dictator would prefer that the employees of the bank not know who he is or what he is doing. Certainly, a greater risk is posed to the extent that the name of a depositor is known throughout the levels of bank employees.

Much of the necessary protection is afforded by the bank secrecy laws of the jurisdiction which make it unlawful to disclose any information concerning a depositor or an account. Some countries provide a narrow exception in the case of serious criminal offenses. Under these rules, the domestic government may obtain limited information in specified cases. Under all other circumstances, it is a crime to divulge any matter concerning an account.

All levels of employees are generally required to sign contracts imposing privacy restrictions, which continue even after employment is terminated. As a practical matter, these rules are taken seriously, and the disclosure exception for criminal matters has been applied in rare cases.

Types of Secret Bank Accounts

To meet the different levels of demand for secrecy, there are generally three types of bank accounts which can be established:

1. Named Account

2. Numbered Account

3. Fictitiously Named Account

Although there is no legal distinction between these accounts concerning the enforcement of bank secrecy laws, there is a difference in the manner that the accounts are handled internally in the bank. In theory, at least, the more restricted the information about the depositor within the bank itself—and the fewer people within the bank who know the true name of the customer—the greater the security of the account.

■ The Named Account

The most common type of account is simply a Named Account. The correct name and address of the depositor is filled in on a bank signature card. As in a U.S. account, the signature card allows bank employees to verify the signature on a withdrawal. In most cases, the financial institution will require identification in the form of a passport, birth certificate, or sometimes a driver's license. Often a letter of reference from the customer's current bank will be necessary. The account application will ask whether the customer wants bank statements held at the institution for pickup or mailed to an address that the customer provides. Communications from the bank may be mailed in plain envelopes, with a return address of a bank manager or employee.

The account application will have the customer designate the signatory on the account. There are several alternatives. The customer can be sole signatory or joint signatory with a spouse or some other person. It can be specified that either signatory can withdraw funds or that the signature of both parties is necessary.

The depositor also specifies the manner for holding the funds and the choice of currency. For example, a deposit in a Bahamian bank can usually be held in U.S. dollars, Swiss francs, or other major currencies. Currencies other than the dollar may pay higher or lower interest rates depending upon the relative stability of that currency. At this moment, interest rates on the Hong Kong dollar are nearly 20 percent per year. However, an investor in this currency runs the risk that the Hong Kong dollar will decline in value and a substantial portion of the deposit may be lost. Diversification of funds among the major currencies is a sound practice, but speculating in order to achieve what appear to be superior returns can be hazardous.

Amounts on deposit, in whichever currency, can be held in a time deposit, which earns interest based on the term of the deposit. The amount of interest is based upon the currency in which the funds are held and the term of the deposit. Dollar accounts will earn interest at the going rate for dollar deposits—meaning the same basic rate as that available in the U.S. If thirty-day certificates of deposit pay 5 percent in the U.S., you will earn approximately that amount in the offshore account.

The variation in the interest rate on dollar denominated accounts is no greater offshore than it is in the U.S. We live in an age where trillions of dollars are moved around the world electronically and instantaneously. If a bank in Bermuda is paying above market rates for dollars (in the form of interest), then that bank will be flooded with deposits quickly. This ability to arbitrage interest rates in the international markets keeps these rates at a uniform level throughout the world.

Brokerage Services Most financial institutions have facilities available for purchasing stocks, bonds, and mutual funds on the U.S. exchanges or other major markets. If you decide that you want to hold shares of IBM in your account, you can direct the bank to buy the stock for you. The bank will perform all of the traditional stock brokerage services. For U.S. stocks, the trades will generally be executed on the U.S. exchanges. However, the customer's name does not appear on the trade. An order to buy 100 shares of IBM is executed under the name of the bank. The physical securities may be delivered to the bank, in its name or can be held in a brokerage account in New York for its account. The bank's internal records show that the customer is the owner, but there is no disclosure of that information. If you want to buy a mutual fund, the purchase will also be in the name of the bank, credited to your account on its books. Your monthly account statement will show the cash balance and the securities which you own.

Most financial institutions will offer you the option of having your funds managed by their investment professionals. If you wish to do so, they will obtain the necessary information about your investment objectives, time horizons, and risk tolerance. If you are not an experienced investor or if you wish to take advantage of a particular expertise, the managed account may satisfy your needs.

Offshore Credit Cards   An additional feature sometimes available with Named Accounts is a credit card, which offers credit up to a specified percentage of the account balance. The advantage of the credit card is that your charges will be reflected only in the name of the bank where you maintain your account. Significant privacy will be accomplished since there will be no charges or records in your individual name. The second advantage is convenience. The funds tucked away safely offshore can be accessed through an ATM or charges at home or anywhere in the world.

HOW OFFSHORE CREDIT CARDS WORK

Steve Smith opens an account at Bank X in the Bahamas. He deposits $50,000. He directs the bank to buy a mutual fund for $25,000 and put the rest in a thirty-day certificate of deposit. He receives a credit card with a limit of $25,000, one half of the equity in the account. The card is issued in the name of Bank X, and the bank is authorized to charge the account for the amount of the purchases plus interest each month. Steve uses his card to withdraw cash when he needs it and to make local purchases. Because the card is in the name of Bank X, there is no record of the charges or withdrawals which Steve makes. Maximum privacy and convenience have been accomplished.

The Limitation on Secrecy—The Dennis Levine Case   The secrecy protection available with the Named Account is based upon the strict laws and banking practices in the jurisdiction. For most people, the protection under this system is adequate for any circumstance which is conceivable. However, it is true that some bank employees will have access to the account agreement with the name and signature of the customer and this human factor may compromise security in some unusual circumstances.

An example of the human factor at work is the case of Dennis Levine. In the early 1980s Levine was a managing director at the investment bank of Drexel Burnham. At the time, the takeover craze was sweeping Wall Street. Acquiring companies often paid well over the current stock price causing the stock of the takeover candidate to zoom skyward. Inevitably, some individuals had access to inside information about which companies were to be acquired before the information was available to the public. As a result, these individuals were in a position to make huge sums of money by buying the stock or options of the target company prior to the public announcement. This insider trading, as tempting as it is, is illegal in the United States.

Because of his position within the investment banking community, Levine had significant access to insider information and was determined to take advantage of every opportunity to profit. To generate additional valuable information, he recruited into his scheme several friends from some of the prominent law firms involved in the takeovers.

Intending to trade based upon these sources, Levine opened an account at the Bahamas office of Bank Leu, a leading Swiss bank. When he wished to purchase stock or options in a company, Levine called his contact at the bank and the transaction was carried out under the name of the bank. After the takeover was announced and the stock rose to the full price, Levine would have the bank sell his position. From 1980 through 1985, Levine traded in the stock of fifty-four companies based on the inside information he acquired. His initial deposit of $100,000 grew to nearly $12 million. Not surprisingly, Levine failed to report this income on his tax returns or pay the tax on this amount.

At the time the Bank Leu account was established, Levine took all significant precautions. Although he executed a signature card in his own name, information about the account was limited to the bank manager, Bruno Pletscher, and several high level employees. His account executive at the bank was Bernhard Meier.

The problem with Levine's careful plan was that after his first few trades resulted in substantial profit, Meier began to piggyback Levine's trades for his own account. That is to say, Meier copied Levine's trades to make himself a profit—a clear breach of every banking policy. Then the broker at Merrill Lynch, in New York, where the trades were executed, joined in the fun and began copying the trades for his account.

The Securities and Exchange Commission eventually put together the pattern of activity in the stock of takeover candidates and was able to trace the source of the trading back to Bank Leu. Although the Bahamas secrecy laws would have shielded the name of Dennis Levine from the SEC, the fact that Meier, an employee of the bank, was engaged in criminal insider trading, caused severe pressure to be exerted on the bank by U.S. authorities. Because Bank Leu felt that Levine had involved it in a criminal scheme, the bank was unwilling to protect him under the circumstances. Levine ultimately pleaded guilty to securities law violations and tax fraud and was sentenced to five years in prison.

The Dennis Levine case is interesting because it demonstrates the limitations of bank secrecy, at least in the Bahamas. This was not simply a matter of a customer depositing funds from an illegal source. Levine had Bank Leu make illegal trades on his behalf, exposing the bank to criminal prosecution in the U.S. No legitimate institution will knowingly risk its reputation and its business for a customer engaged in criminal activity.

Secondly, banks are composed of human employees. Under most circumstances, the bank secrecy laws will be effective in preventing any unwanted disclosure. And in fact, over the last fifty years, with millions of depositors in the offshore jurisdictions, there have been only a handful of cases of disclosure. But because there are humans involved, mistakes can be made.

■ **Numbered Accounts**

Some banks offer Numbered Accounts as an alternative to the Named Account. The purpose of the Numbered Account is to reduce to a bare minimum the bank employees who have access to the name of the account holder.

The classic Numbered Account is legendary in the popular culture, as expressed in countless movies and books. Every self-respecting spy, mercenary, or other financially astute international criminal always demands a substantial advance deposit in his Numbered Account before performing the requested services. The Numbered Account is like home base. It represents the ultimate in safety and security. Funds tucked away in the Numbered Account are home free.

In this case the reality is fairly close to the popular conception. Numbered Accounts do offer increased privacy. In the usual case, the customer's name and address will be provided on the account opening agreement together with the customer's signature. The difference with the Named Account is that the information, other than the account number, will not be entered in the general bank system which most employees can access. Instead, the account will be assigned for personal handling to an individual account manager. The file with the customer's name is maintained separately from the Named Accounts, with access available only to key personnel. Normally, the investment of the funds and any withdrawals or deposits are based upon some agreed form of communication between the account manager and the customer. When the communication is not face to face, such as by telephone or written instruction, a secret code will be applied in addition to the account number.

Unlike the Named Account, the true Numbered Account requires a higher degree of special handling which not all banks are equipped to supply. And since every bank is justifiably averse to providing special services without compensation, the Numbered Account will be more expensive to maintain and may only be available to those with substantial sums to deposit.

As a word of caution, an offer of an alleged Numbered Account in Antigua, Nevis, or Belize should be met with a high degree of skepticism. Numbered Accounts are the exclusive province of the banks with strict standards and specialized training for management and account executives. These banks can generally be found in Switzerland, Liechtenstein, and Luxembourg, with a tradition and culture of personal service and professional expertise. Caribbean branches of the European banks may also offer properly skilled and trained staff who provide high quality private banking services. Any prospective customer should carefully investigate the reputation and performance of any offshore bank before placing lifetime savings in their care.

■ The Fictitiously Named Account

In addition to the Named Account and the Numbered Account, it is possible to tighten the secrecy attributes of the relationship one notch further. In a Fictitiously Named Account, the true name of the customer is not revealed. Although the bank manager knows the real name of the customer, the account opening agreement contains a fictitious name so that there is no written evidence of the account owner. If Steve Smith wanted to open such an account, the actual name on the agreement could be John Doe–Account Number 1234. In all communications, the customer would identify himself as John Doe–Account Number 1234. Again written and telephone directions would contain the previously agreed code. As with a Numbered Account, the Fictitiously Named Account requires a high degree of sensitive handling by the bank and is not generally available to the public except by special arrangement.

Practical Problems with
Secret Accounts—Too Much Secrecy

A serious real life problem with any secrecy account is the death of the customer. Although it is possible to provide for an alternate signatory in the event of death, this only works if the bank is in fact advised of the death.

For example, Steve Smith opens an account and specifies that his wife Betty Smith will become the signatory upon Steve's death. Twenty years later Steve dies, having forgotten to tell Betty about the account. The bank has no knowledge of Steve's death, and so the account just sits there. The money is out of the family forever.

What if Steve does tell Betty but she dies before him? Again, on Steve's subsequent death nobody knows about the account, and so no one claims it. We have seen this problem played out in real life with dramatic consequences. In the 1930s and 1940s, many European Jews deposited their savings in Swiss banks to protect them from the Nazis. When these individuals later perished in the Holocaust, surviving family members often had no knowledge about the account and the money went unclaimed. No one knows the total amount which was lost but estimates range from $50 million to $5 billion. Only recently, because of intense international pressure, have the Swiss government and the banks attempted to identify these accounts and distribute the funds to the surviving relatives.

In our example, if Steve wants to make sure that his family claims the money, he will have to make provisions so that the executor of his estate is or becomes aware of the account in the event of Steve's death. The executor, in possession of the death certificate and the proper authorization, will be able to assume control of the account on behalf of Steve's estate. However, the proper information must be available—i.e. the name of the bank and the account information—and that requires arrangements and a mechanism for disclosure during lifetime.

■ The Perjury Problem

Besides these practical problems associated with the death of the account owner, from a legal standpoint it is not advisable to hold a bank account in an individual name. Remember, the objective of any sound asset protection plan is to maintain control while removing legal ownership from your name.

An offshore account, just like your home and other savings, should be placed within a structure which provides the appropriate degree of legal protection. If you are questioned under oath, you must tell the truth about what you own and how it is held. The proper legal structure allows you to tell the truth and still have your property protected from a claim.

Privacy Structures

The most popular arrangements for holding overseas accounts are the Asset Protection Trust and the International Business Corporation.

The APT is a flexible and convenient format for holding offshore assets such as bank and brokerage accounts, foreign real estate, and interests in other business entities. Financial privacy is achieved because the laws of the country governing the APT generally do not require disclosure of the names of the settlor, beneficiary, or protector. For instance, in the Cook Islands, the name of the trust is registered with the government, but all other information is held in confidence by the trust company. The trust document itself is also held in secrecy. If Steve Smith creates a trust, his name will be known to the trust company, but there will be no public record of his connection with the trust. In the Cayman Islands, a trust can be formed without any registration process.

Accounts can be opened in the name of the APT and, subject to local law or bank policy, the name of the settlor and beneficiary need not be disclosed. The trust can buy and sell stocks and make investments anywhere in the world—with complete anonymity for the owner.

The trust structure allows a diverse group of assets and businesses to be consolidated within a single entity for efficient administration and ultimate distribution. When everything is held under one roof, management and control are greatly simplified. The trust company is familiar with all of the assets, where they are held and what needs to be done. In the event of the settlor's death, the trust carries on in the manner specified in the trust agreement. Administration can be continued by the trust company or assets may be distributed to the surviving spouse or family members as the settlor provided. Trust assets are not subject to court probate and the transfer of ownership is instantaneous—without interruption or complexity.

International Business Corporations   Offshore business and investment activity is usually conducted with an entity known as the International Business Corporation. The IBC may be used to hold and segregate Dangerous Assets, located overseas, that we would not own directly in the APT.

Also, it is sometimes more convenient to open a bank or brokerage account in the name of the corporation rather than in the trust. Corporations are recognized and permitted by law in every country. There is a standard set of rules which govern the operation and management of a corporation, and all banks have proper account opening procedures already in place.

Although it is getting to be less of a problem, for a number of years many of the major banks were not familiar with or knowledgeable about the APT structure and preferred that the accounts be opened in the name of a corporation. This is partially due to the fact that except for the British Commonwealth countries, the prevailing civil law in Europe does not recognize the legal entity that we call a trust. Banks which do not have a previous relationship with the trust company or the settlor will often insist on the corporate account with well-established account opening and maintenance procedures. In these situations, an IBC can be formed with shares issued to or held by the APT. Most of the tax haven jurisdictions have enacted legislation enabling the formation of IBCs.

It is not necessary to bank or conduct business in the country where the IBC is formed. In fact, the major advantage of the IBC is its portability. An IBC formed in the Bahamas can open a bank account in Switzerland or any other country, including the United States. The bank will ask to see the articles of incorporation and a corporate resolution by the directors authorizing the opening of the account and appointing a person to act as signatory for the corporation on the account. With that information and proper identification for the signatory, an IBC account can be opened anywhere in the world.

The Cayman Islands, the Bahamas, and the British Virgin Islands are no tax jurisdictions which allow complete secrecy of ownership for corporations. To set up a company in these jurisdictions, one of the many local law firms or trust companies is contacted. It will file the necessary corporate registration to create the company. The firm can also serve as the sole member of the board of directors. If anonymity is required, the shares can be issued in bearer form. That means that no name is registered on the share certificate. Instead, whoever holds the certificate becomes the owner of the company.

To avoid the possible difficulties arising from lost or stolen shares, the certificates are registered in the name of the law firm or trust company. It then holds the shares under an agreement to serve as nominee for the true owner. Any necessary corporate documents or even bank accounts are signed by the nominee as instructed by the beneficial owner. If the APT is to hold the shares, it can maintain bearer shares or the shares can be registered in the name of the trust.

Contrast the IBC with a corporation established in the United States. In the U.S. the names and addresses of the officers and directors of the corporation must be publicly filed in the state where it is formed. Shares must be registered in the name of the true owner. A stock register is required to be maintained, listing the name and address of each shareholder. The stock register can be subpoenaed by any government agency or by the plaintiff in a lawsuit. The individuals behind any domestic U.S. company are readily identifiable to any third party investigating the matter. We can create privacy for a U.S. corporation by using a domestic Privacy Trust. But for those with funds or business interests overseas, the IBC is a popular approach.

KEY FACTORS FOR CHOOSING THE APPROPRIATE LOCATION FOR AN IBC

- The absence of taxes on IBC income.

- A simplified registration process.

- Anonymity of ownership.

- Experienced and reliable local trust companies to perform routine administration.

- The costs and fees for services.

Summary

Personal privacy and confidentiality in financial matters is protected by law and tradition in many countries throughout the world. In Switzerland, Austria, and several smaller nations, bank secrecy laws forbid unauthorized disclosure of customer information. In contrast, information about your financial account in the United States is readily available to government authorities, commercial marketers, and those involved in litigation.

Individuals who wish to create a sophisticated level of privacy and asset protection, beyond that which can be accomplished with a strictly domestic plan, often take advantage of the opportunities presented by the bank secrecy accounts. An Asset Protection Trust or International Business Corporation with an overseas account is a popular plan for holding and investing funds outside of the U.S. banking and legal system.

CHAPTER THIRTEEN

How to Avoid Tax Traps and Scams

WE HAVE DISCUSSED THE ADVANTAGES of the Privacy Trust with domestic and offshore strategies for accomplishing a high level of financial privacy and asset protection. But these arrangements are subject to abuse in a number of circumstances—involving tax issues and fraudulent transfers—and in this chapter we want to alert you to the dangers we have seen. We will provide a concise and accurate explanation of how the important rules apply to the various strategies so that you can protect yourself from devious schemes.

Popular Delusions about Tax Issues

Misinformation on the Internet

The Internet is not only a powerful source of information for and about you—it represents a dangerous tool for distributing misleading and fraudulent claims. The system allows for massive global dissemination of misinformation to unwary individuals, who have no specific training in a topic and little ability to separate the truth from the lies.

In the pre-Internet days information was disseminated through books and magazines. When you wanted to research a topic, you went to a book store or the library. The editor of the publication reviewed the material for accuracy before it was published. At least in theory, some intellectual or academic standards were applied to texts on legal matters in determining whether the material should be published. Similarly, the book store or library had some criteria for deciding whether to carry the publication. The effect of this system was a level of discrimination which favored knowledgeable sources with ascertainable credentials.

Now we have the Internet as the preeminent reference source for information on any topic. As a consequence, there is no level of discrimination applied. Anybody can say anything they want. Don't want to pay taxes anymore? No doubt you'll find someone on the Internet who will tell you to declare yourself a sovereign individual and withdraw from the U.S. tax system. Don't like the IRS? Again, on the Internet, you'll find advice that claims the income tax is unconstitutional and can't legally be collected from you. Now anyone can publicly misstate the law for their own profit—without legal responsibility or repercussions. In fact, the more bizarre and outrageous the premise, it seems the greater the following that is attracted and the more money the promoters are able to earn.

Tax Evasion

One argument, popular on numerous Web sites, is that there is a legal or Constitutional justification for not paying U.S. income taxes. The basis of this theory is not decipherable since every conceivable challenge to the income tax has been soundly rejected by the U.S. Supreme Court—which is the ultimate interpreter of the law in our country. But many people don't realize that there is a difference between what they want to believe and what really is true.

There is no *legal* justification for not paying taxes. You can try a moral argument that the government doesn't deserve the money. Or you might rely on the practical argument that you won't get caught if you don't pay your taxes. Either of these positions makes more sense than the claim that the government has no legal authority to collect taxes.

Phony Tax Strategies

Another group of scam artists acknowledges that the income tax is legal but maintain that there are completely legitimate methods to avoid it. These claims are a little more imaginative and significantly more devious because they intentionally take advantage of the fact that most people are not familiar with the Internal Revenue Code and how the tax law operates. These claims appeal to people's greed and gullibility and their desire to believe a story that makes them happy—no matter how implausible.

For example, on most days we speak to at least one prospective client, who says that he wants to avoid taxes by setting up an irrevocable trust, an offshore corporation, or a private bank account. These prospects say, "I've paid millions of taxes over the last twenty years and I've had enough. I don't want to pay any more taxes." We explain how the law works and that none of those schemes will legally save him a nickel in taxes. But the prospective client tells us that he read a book about private offshore banks or he spoke to an "offshore consultant" or even an attorney, who told him that for $30,000 in fees he could set up a structure and not have to pay taxes anymore. It's clear that he doesn't believe us when we try to discourage him.

Our observation is that most individuals will fool themselves into believing that a lie is the truth if the lie provides them with some positive economic benefit or emotional comfort. It's not even a conscious effort. Given a choice between two alternative explanations of events, the mind will choose to believe the explanation that provides the greatest degree of comfort.

The same process occurs even when one explanation is irrational and the other is sensible. If the irrational argument offers a more appealing result, it will be accepted. The husband whose wife walks in while he is in bed with his girlfriend says, "Honey, who are you going to believe—me or your lying eyes?" The point is don't let yourself be fooled by anyone who tells you that he has an easy or even a complicated plan for you to avoid taxes on your income.

Can you get away without paying taxes? Maybe. Unless of course the promoter of the deal is arrested—which is likely since he is advertising his services in every newspaper in America and across the planet on the Internet. And when he is caught, he will try to save himself from going to jail by giving up *your* name, address, and account number. Then you will be caught and unless you can make a deal to stay out of jail by giving information about someone else, you will be the one mopping floors in the penitentiary.

Pure Trusts and Common Law Trusts

There has also been extremely heavy promotion of a concept that is referred to as a "Pure Trust" or "Common Law Trust." The promoters claim that these so-called strategies offer privacy, asset protection, and tax savings. There is typically a garbled reference to sovereign individuals and declaring yourself free of the tax system. Sometimes they claim that they have uncovered a loophole in the tax law—which nobody else knows about. They usually direct you to an 800 number which provides testimonials from satisfied customers about how they don't pay taxes anymore.

It may be true that these people aren't paying taxes—but they certainly should be. The concept of these trusts is complete nonsense. It is made up out of thin air. There is no legal support for these claims, and their sole purpose is to defraud innocent people out of their money.

The IRS and the Department of Justice have formed a special task force to investigate the promoters and users of these trusts. In April 1997, the IRS issued Notice 97-24 which states that the IRS is actively examining abusive trust arrangements which purport to reduce or eliminate income taxes. Individuals using these tactics are subject to both civil and criminal penalties. A dispute with the government on this or any other similar tax issue will result in financial ruin for you and your family so we advise you to stay clear of the promoters of these schemes.

Taxation of Privacy Trusts

The Privacy Trust, which we have proposed, will not produce any net change in your overall income tax. It is typically structured as a "grantor trust" so that all of the income is taxed to you on your personal return. The purpose of the Privacy Trust is to maximize privacy and asset protection; it is not intended to provide any income tax advantages. Because of this, you are assured that Congress and the IRS will not be investigating or regulating this privacy strategy and no unfavorable or unintended consequences will be produced for you.

Taxation of Offshore Activities

We have talked about strategies involving overseas accounts and offshore trusts and corporations. Now we will see how they are taxed in the U.S. and whether there are any tax advantages to using these strategies.

U.S. Taxation of Citizens and Residents

The basic premise of U.S. tax law is that *every citizen and resident of the United States is subject to income tax on his or her worldwide income.* This applies in several meaningful ways. If you are a citizen, you must pay income tax regardless of where you live. For example, if you live and work in Saudi Arabia, you must still pay tax on your income to the United States. Similarly, if you are a resident of the U.S., you will pay tax on amounts you earn anywhere in the world. Under this system, wherever you earn this income—in the U.S. or outside the country—the amount is still subject to tax.

This rule means that income earned in an overseas account is subject to U.S. tax in the year in which it is earned. *When* the funds are brought into the country is not relevant. If you open an overseas account in 1999 and earn $3,000 in interest, that amount is taxable on your return in 1999. It doesn't matter whether you bring the $3,000 back into the U.S. It is taxable in the year it is earned—not the year it is returned to the U.S.

An entity that is formed in the U.S., such as a corporation, a Limited Liability Company, or a partnership, is treated like a resident individual. It is taxed on its worldwide income.

The scheme for taxing U.S. residents and citizens should be clear to you now. Everything you earn—anywhere you earn it—is subject to U.S. tax.

Taxation of Foreign
Corporations and Individuals

How does this system apply to foreign companies and individuals who are not residents in the U.S.? If a corporation is formed in another country, when is it subject to U.S. tax? That is a more complicated matter, but here are the general rules. We will refer to both foreign corporations and nonresident individuals as Nonresidents.

1. If a Nonresident is engaged in a business in the U.S., it is subject to tax on the income associated with that business. Many companies do business all over the world, including the U.S. If the company is a Nonresident, it will be subject to tax in the U.S. only on the income earned from its U.S. business.

   For example, a French perfume maker sells its product in many countries. It opens a retail store in the U.S. and sells the perfume to customers of the store. The company is a Nonresident, subject to tax in the U.S. only on the business that it does here (from the retail store). Its income from operations outside the U.S. will be taxed by the French government.

2. Nonresidents which are not engaged in a business in the U.S. must pay taxes only on certain types of fixed income from the U.S—generally rents, royalties, interest, and dividends. For these types of payments, a tax at the rate of 30 percent must be withheld and paid to the IRS by the person or company making the payment to the Nonresident. For example, if you borrow money from a Bahamas Bank, you will have to withhold and pay to the IRS 30 percent of each interest payment you make on the loan.

This amount of the withholding tax can be reduced, possibly to zero, if the amount is paid to a resident of a country which is a party to a treaty with the U.S. That is because that country will apply its own tax to the income when it is received. The U.S does not make these treaty arrangements with tax havens or low tax jurisdictions.

3. The Nonresident which is not engaged in a business in the U.S. is not subject to tax on interest from bank deposits and capital gains. Nonresidents are free to deposit funds in U.S. banks without being taxed on the interest income. This system encourages a free flow of money into the banking system. Similarly, capital gains such as from stock sales are not taxed—encouraging investment in our equities markets. Gains from the sale of U.S. real estate do not fall under this rule. Capital gains from the sale of real estate are subject to tax in the U.S.

To summarize these rules, Nonresidents only pay tax on U.S. business income and some types of passive income such as rents, interest, and royalties. Interest on bank deposits and capital gains (other than from real estate) is not taxable. Conversely, a Nonresident which has no U.S. business income and no rents, royalties, or interest from this country does not pay taxes in the U.S.

These rules appear to leave the door open to some relatively easy planning for weary U.S. taxpayers. Why not form a foreign corporation in a tax haven such as the Bahamas, transfer all of your savings into the corporation, and let the corporation earn tax free interest and capital gains?

The answer is that the IRS is one step ahead of you; this technique is prohibited. In general, if U.S. shareholders own more than 50 percent of the stock of a foreign corporation, they are treated as receiving their proportionate share or corporate income each year. You can't get around this rule by having relatives or related entities hold your shares for you. For tax purposes, you are treated as owning any shares held by close relatives or entities that you own.

Since the taxability of the income of a foreign corporation depends upon whether the shareholders are U.S. residents, you can understand why all of the tax haven countries offer bearer shares or other forms of anonymous ownership. *If the identity of the owners cannot be determined, how can they be taxed?* Offshore financial institutions don't issue 1099s so the earnings of the company are not reported to the U.S. or any other government. When anonymous ownership is coupled with the bank secrecy rules, taxing the income of these companies remains a challenge for the tax authorities in any country.

Taxation of Foreign Trusts

A foreign trust is taxed in a different manner than a corporation. The basic rule is that a trust set up by a U.S. person with one or more U.S beneficiaries is treated as a grantor trust for tax purposes—just like the Privacy Trust. The tax is no higher or lower than it would have been. Income earned on an overseas bank account or a stock sale will be taxable on the U.S. return of the settlor. There need not be any distribution from the trust. The income is reported when it is earned.

Reporting Requirement
for Foreign Trusts

A potentially significant development involves new legislation designed to increase the information available to the government concerning the creation and transfer of property to a foreign trust. In August 1996, as part of the Small Business Investment Act, legislation was enacted which specified filing and reporting requirements for all foreign trusts.

Under the new law, a foreign trust is defined as any trust which is not (1) subject to the primary supervision of a U.S. court; and (2) controlled by one or more U.S. fiduciaries with respect to substantial decisions concerning the trust. A trust that is not subject to the jurisdiction of a U.S. court and controlled by a U.S. trustee will be classified as a foreign trust, subject to the new reporting requirements.

Reporting for
Asset Protection Trusts

An Asset Protection Trust can be designed to avoid the new filing requirements. Since assets are in the U.S., under the control of a U.S. trustee, the trust will be treated as a domestic trust. At the point that assets have been transferred to the overseas trust account or the U.S trustees no longer have exclusive control over trust assets, it will then be considered to be a foreign trust and compliance with the reporting requirements will become necessary.

Avoiding
Fraudulent Transfers

When you establish a Privacy Trust or develop any strategy for privacy and asset protection, it is important to understand the laws regarding *fraudulent transfers*. In general, transfers which are made to avoid paying a debt or an obligation can be set aside by a court. In serious cases, a fraudulent transfer can result in civil or criminal penalties.

For as long as there have been commercial transactions, people have attempted to conceal their ownership of property to defeat the claims of their creditors. Concealment may take the form of physically hiding money or jewelry, or it may take the form of "gifts" to friendly parties or relatives. Usually, such "gifts" are accompanied by secret agreements to return the property after the trouble has passed.

In an effort to protect creditors from this endless game of hide and seek, English speaking courts have, for approximately 400 years, sought to invalidate transfers made by a person with the intent to defraud his creditors. Any transfer of property that is proved to be a fraudulent transfer will be ignored, and the property will be treated as if it is still owned by the debtor. That means the property will then be available to be seized by the judgment creditor. This law is currently embodied in the Uniform Fraudulent Conveyance Act and the Uniform Fraudulent Transfer Act, which are similar in coverage and either of which is in effect in most states.

When Is a Transfer Fraudulent?

A transfer is subject to being set aside as a "fraudulent conveyance" in at least four circumstances:

1. The transfer is made with the "actual intent to hinder, delay, or defraud any creditor of the debtor."

2. The transfer does not involve the receipt of "reasonably equivalent value" *and* the person making the transfer becomes insolvent (or was insolvent prior to the exchange).

3. The transfer does not include the receipt of "reasonably equivalent value" *and* the person making the transfer knows (or should have known) that with his remaining resources he will be unable to pay future debts.

4. The transfer is without "reasonably equivalent value" *and* the person making the transfer continues to operate a business with assets that are "unreasonably small" in relation to typical existing or proposed business transactions.

A "transfer" encompasses not only the disposition of assets but taking on additional debt or obligations without receiving an equivalent benefit. For example, giving a friend a mortgage on your home without receiving the cash loan proceeds could qualify as a fraudulent transfer.

If you make a transfer of your property—attempting to keep it away from someone with a claim against you—it will certainly be considered a fraudulent transfer. Most commonly, if you are being sued or you are about to be sued, you cannot transfer your assets to avoid paying the judgment. Anytime you transfer your property into a Privacy Trust or other asset protection plan you must make sure that you have retained access to sufficient funds or income so that you will be able to meet your outstanding obligations when they become due.

The Privacy Trust is a unique and powerful legal weapon. If you avoid the promoters who offer to hide income, evade taxes, or defraud creditors, you will find that the Privacy Trust can create significant privacy and asset protection advantages that cannot be duplicated by any other plan.

CHAPTER FOURTEEN

Questions and Answers About Financial Privacy

What information can someone find out about me?

Most financial and personal information can be located through Internet databases. An investigator who is hired to search for your assets will generally locate bank and brokerage accounts with account numbers and balances, real estate in any part of the country, business ownership, and vehicles such as boats, cars, and aircraft.

Personal identifying information includes your name, aliases, current and previous addresses, telephone number, mother's maiden name, Social Security number, driver's license number, and birth date. Additional data include names of relatives, bankruptcies, civil filings, tax liens, judgments, UCC filings, stock ownership, names of other household members, neighborhood demographics, and a list of up to thirty neighbors' names and telephone numbers.

Investigators also can obtain your telephone records with the names of each person or business you called, your credit card charge receipts and balances, employment history, and family income.

Based on this information, a personal information report can be prepared—often more than 100 pages—which provides a detailed and comprehensive picture of who you are, what you own, how much you are worth, what you do for a living, and how much you make.

Who uses this information?

Insurance companies often use database information to examine their underwriting risk and to detect fraud in a variety of cases. Lenders compile these reports to determine whether to make or extend a loan to a particular customer. Federal and state law enforcement agencies use these services to locate witnesses and suspects and to detect money laundering and evidence of other financial crimes.

Most commonly, the financial information and personal data is used by lawyers in connection with proposed litigation. It is now standard practice for an attorney to investigate the available assets and background of a potential defendant prior to filing a lawsuit.

What dangers are created by the availability of my personal financial data?

Access to your personal financial information encourages lawsuits, claims, disputes, and threats from those who want what you have. Instinctively, most people realize that keeping quiet about personal financial matters is the smart thing to do.

Talking about what you have and how much you make can invite envy or arouse greed in others. There are plenty of "bad guys" out there. If they know you have some money, you become a target for their schemes. Telemarketers, con men, disgruntled business associates, employees, and even family members may try to take some or all of what you have.

Filing a lawsuit against you is now the most popular and effective scheme for someone to take advantage of you and get your money. When you are sued, you face a threat of serious financial loss. Because defending even the most frivolous lawsuit is expensive and the outcome is always unpredictable, you will be forced to pay a significant amount to settle the case. While mobsters use the threat of physical harm to extort protection money from their victims, a lawyer may use the legal system and the threat of a lawsuit to extort money from innocent defendants who would rather pay than risk financial ruin.

What strategies are available to protect my financial privacy?

There is no practical method for restricting access to much of the personal identifying information about you maintained in the databases. Your name, address, and Social Security number have been widely distributed. As they say, the toothpaste is out of the tube.

But you can make sure that—even with this information—nobody can find out what you own. You can protect the privacy of your bank and brokerage accounts, your real estate, and your business interests with a Privacy Trust. That will eliminate most serious and potentially damaging consequences of these privacy intrusions.

What is a Privacy Trust?

The Privacy Trust is a type of trust, designed as a convenient and practical strategy for achieving an excellent level of financial privacy. Your ownership of real estate, bank accounts, brokerage accounts, mutual funds, and business interests can be legally concealed within the trust arrangement. Investigators, lawyers, and the database services—attempting to gather information about what you own—will not successfully locate assets held by the Privacy Trust. You can effectively restrict access to your financial records to those whom you choose.

In addition to these privacy advantages, depending upon the type of plan which is created, significant asset protection and estate planning goals can also be accomplished.

Are there any legal restrictions on the use of the Privacy Trust?

The Privacy Trust cannot be used to evade taxes or defraud a creditor. Also, the trust cannot be used for money laundering, which is concealing the proceeds of a criminal activity. Whenever you are required by law to provide financial information under oath, you must make complete and truthful disclosure in answering any questions presented to you.

What are the features of the Privacy Trust–Plan #1

This arrangement is designed primarily to establish privacy for *domestic* assets—U.S. real estate and financial accounts in local banks and brokerage firms. The trust is opened with a local trust company, which meets your standards of reliability. Property and accounts are transferred into the name of the trust. You continue to manage and deal with the assets—just like before. You can buy or sell stocks or other investments without interference. Account agreements and real estate documents are signed by the trust company—as you instruct.

Can I withdraw money from the trust?

The trust does not diminish your ability to spend, sell, or borrow against any assets. If you want funds from your account, simply instruct the trust company to issue a check to you. If you use the income from an investment account for living expenses, you can arrange to have regular monthly checks delivered to you.

Can I sell my property?

Your property can be sold or refinanced at any time. The trust company will sign any necessary documents which you present. The sale proceeds can be distributed to you by the trust or reinvested according to your wishes.

Are there any estate planning advantages?

The trust can be designed to accomplish all of your important estate planning goals. Probate can be avoided for all of the assets in the trust. Estate taxes will be minimized, and the property will be passed in the manner you determine. If you have young children, you may wish to have the property remain in the trust, with the money used to care for them until they are grown. You can name a close friend or family member to act as sole or co-trustee—with or without the initial trust company.

How long does this trust last?

The Privacy Trust can be revoked or changed at any time. If you no longer need it, you can cancel the trust—or you can simply take over as the sole trustee.

Are there any tax benefits with this arrangement?

Your income tax will not be changed. The trust will be treated as a revocable, grantor trust. All income and expense will continue to be reported on your personal tax return. Mortgage interest, dividends, capital gains, and losses will be included directly in your tax calculation. Transfers of property to and from the trust do not create any tax consequences. These transfers are ignored for tax purposes.

How do I know that I can trust the trust company?

All trust companies must be approved and licensed by the state where they do business. They are subject to many of the same strict regulatory requirements as banks and other financial institutions. Trust companies must be adequately capitalized and are required to maintain a bond to insure customers against negligence or fraud. The trust companies are often affiliates or subsidiaries of large national financial service firms such as banks or title companies. Trillions of dollars in the United States are managed or controlled by trust companies, and the risks are no greater than with any other type of financial institution.

The legitimate concern, which you should have, is the quality of the service offered by the trust company. You will want your questions answered and your instructions carried out promptly and accurately. When you want a check to be written or a document signed, the service must be efficient and convenient.

In our experience, many trust companies do not perform their responsibilities with the necessary level of diligence and competency. Employees often lack training or motivation and annoying delays and inaccuracies typically plague the relationship.

However, there are a select group of firms which specialize in administering Privacy Trusts—with highly skilled, experienced, and responsive trust officers. These are the only trust companies that we use to create our privacy strategies.

Does the Privacy Trust–Plan #1 provide any asset protection benefits?

Access to your financial information can *encourage* lawsuits and claims against you from a variety of sources. If a potential adversary knows what you have and how much you are worth, your risk of a lawsuit increases dramatically. Holding your property within a Privacy Trust effectively conceals your ownership. Without reachable and available assets, you will no longer be an attractive target for a lawsuit.

If you are sued, despite these precautions, the Privacy Trust–Plan #1 will not protect trust assets from a judgment. Property held in a revocable trust can be seized if you lose the case. Although this plan is excellent for privacy purposes, if your goal is asset protection you should consider one of the other strategies.

Can you describe the Privacy Trust–Plan #2?

This plan is designed to combine asset protection benefits with a high level of financial privacy. Instead of holding accounts and property directly in the trust, assets are transferred to entities which provide legal protection from potential claims. Family Limited Partnerships and Limited Liability Companies offer this type of protection. The ownership of the entity is placed in the Privacy Trust.

How does this arrangement create asset protection?

FLPs and LLCs are considered to be separate and distinct legal entities—apart from their owners. The law provides that the assets of an LLC or FLP cannot be seized to satisfy a judgment against the owner.

How does the plan create financial privacy?

The Privacy Trust, as the owner of the entity, acts on its behalf to open accounts and execute documents. For example, your brokerage account can be placed in an LLC. The Privacy Trust is the sole member—holding all of the ownership interests.

The trust company signs the account opening agreement—using its federal tax identification number—and acts as signatory on the LLC account. The account in the LLC is legally protected from claims against you. In addition, your name and Social Security number do not appear on the account. There is no information to connect you to the ownership. You have successfully concealed your interest in the account.

Real estate can be purchased or transferred in the name of the LLC. Title to the property is held in the LLC, which is owned by the Privacy Trust. Your name is no longer connected with the ownership of the property. A search of the databases and public records for your real estate will not reveal this property.

How is Privacy Trust–Plan #3 different from Plan #2?

Plan #3 is known as the *Safety Valve* plan. It provides an extra layer of protection that some people consider important.

In Plan #3, we add to the structure the capability to move funds out of the U.S. at any time. With this strategy, amounts can be transferred into an overseas trust account, protected by favorable asset protection and privacy laws.

Where do funds go that are sent overseas?

Any amounts transferred from your U.S. accounts would go to a trust account that you have previously established. You can choose the overseas bank (often a large Swiss or Caribbean bank) and the terms of the account. You may have the trust company act as signatory, or you *and* the trust company can be designated as signatories. Funds are then held or invested according to your wishes.

What is the role of the Asset Protection Trust?

In Plan #3, the APT is added as the beneficiary of the Privacy Trust. Just as in Plan #2, accounts and real estate can be maintained locally, usually in the LLC—with excellent privacy and protection. Property can be transferred to the APT, in the future, if the need arises. The APT has four specially designed protection features:

1. **A creditor is only permitted to reach assets which are "owned" by the debtor.** Property transferred to the APT is legally owned by the trust—not by you. The trust is a separate and distinct legal entity. A creditor cannot seize the assets of the trust to satisfy your debt.

2. **The Anti-Duress Clause protects your property from any U.S. court orders.** The trust agreement provides that the trust company cannot respond to any instructions which are issued by you under court order or any legal compulsion. The trust company will not authorize any disposition of trust assets unless instructed to do so by you acting under your own free will. This is known as the Anti-Duress Clause, and it is an essential provision in every APT.

3. **The Asset Protection Trust has one trustee not subject to U.S. jurisdiction.** All APTs are required to have a trustee whose business is located in the country whose laws govern the trust. The trust company is not subject to the jurisdiction of any U.S. court or agency and cannot be compelled by a court to perform any acts or release any information concerning the trust or its assets.

4. **Trust assets can be transferred to an overseas trust account if additional protection is desired.** In the typical situation, all of your assets will remain at your local financial institution. However, the trust provides the option for you to transfer

funds to the overseas trust account to take advantage of more favorable asset protection and privacy laws.

Is it necessary to transfer money offshore to achieve a high level of privacy?

The Privacy Trust is an effective technique for protecting financial privacy without the necessity of an offshore account. Using the Privacy Trust allows you to keep your account at Charles Schwab and Co., or E-Trade, or wherever you prefer. It is easy to operate and maintain and provides a convenient alternative to an offshore account.

At some point in the future, new laws or regulations may be issued which impair the effectiveness of the Privacy Trust. But for now, it is a fine and complete solution to a troublesome and dangerous problem.

Are there any benefits to an offshore account?

An overseas account with a good bank, in a country with strict bank secrecy laws, is an alternative to the Privacy Trust. Although it is more cumbersome and expensive to administer than the Privacy Trust, individuals with sophisticated and complex financial matters sometimes choose to maintain some or all of their funds in an overseas account.

One advantage of the offshore account is that the quality of service in a European bank is usually superior to that available in the U.S. If you want both confidentiality and attentive service— and are willing to pay for it—an overseas account may be the appropriate solution.

An overseas account can also play an important role in an asset protection plan. When the account is held in a properly structured APT, the funds are outside the jurisdiction of a U.S court and are protected from potential claims.

Do I need to protect the information on my personal computer?

Your privacy plan may be perfect from a legal standpoint and impossible to penetrate by an outsider. The weakness of your plan will be your own records, notes, and correspondences that you have created concerning the plan. In most cases, the *only* way that your private matters will be disclosed is through your own words— as you have written them on your computer. These records, stored in computer files, provide the most direct and convenient access to all of the personal and financial matters that you are trying to keep confidential. All of your "smoking guns" are right there, on your computer.

Your computer files often include all of your important personal and business records. For example, Quicken and other popular software programs consolidate accounting, banking, investments, tax, and financial information into a single combined package— convenient for you and also for anybody who wants to learn all about you. If you bank online, trade stocks online, or follow your portfolio on the Internet, a trail is created and a record is stored in your computer's memory of Web sites you have visited and files which have been downloaded. Word processing files may contain highly sensitive correspondence with your bank or brokerage firm that you would not want others to discover. E-mail communications with your lawyer, offshore banker, or trust company will often provide the only evidence of the existence of your privacy plan together with detailed asset and account information.

E-mail has largely replaced fax and conventional mail as the preferred means of communication. Messages tend to be less formal, more conversational, and more revealing than traditional written documents. Everyone from Bill Gates to Monica Lewinsky has now seen their private e-mail messages—stored on their own computers—come back to haunt them in serious litigation or through embarrassing revelations in the news media.

Most people don't take adequate security precautions to protect their computer information from snooping eyes. We know of hundreds of cases where months of careful planning was foiled by carelessly guarded files or computer records.

Anyone who lives or works around your office, your employees, and even family members can find your private files in your computer if they are motivated to do so. A potential adversary with a serious interest in what you do can usually accomplish an unauthorized search of your home or office computer quickly and quietly. Your computer records can be seized by the government in a civil or criminal investigation, and they certainly will be subpoenaed if you are involved in a lawsuit.

Deleting sensitive or unwanted files does not eliminate the information from your computer and is not the answer to the problem. The "delete" key merely removes the file name from the directory. You may think that you have erased the data from the computer but in fact, it's still there—stored in many different files in the computer's memory.

The files may be invisible to you but professional investigators with the proper training and the right software tools can uncover the deleted files without great difficulty. A surreptitious search or a court ordered inspection of your computer hard drive can recover visible and deleted e-mail, word processing files, and accounting information which may provide incriminating or embarrassing evidence against you. Recovered e-mail messages and files, long since deleted and forgotten, can cause serious damage to your case and your carefully constructed plans.

What steps should I take to protect the information on my computer?

A privacy plan is not complete without a strategy to protect the confidential information which you have stored on your computer. Just as we have concealed the ownership of bank accounts, real estate, and investments, it is necessary to ensure that your personal computer records do not reveal the information that you are trying to protect. Financial records as well as personal and business communications must be secured against unauthorized searches of your computer.

A privacy plan for your computer records involves creating the capability for encrypting, hiding, and destroying sensitive files that contain confidential material.

Encryption means scrambling the words and numbers on a document so that it is indecipherable by anyone who doesn't have the correct password or the code. Software now allows you to powerfully encrypt the contents of any or all of your documents with an unbreakable code by a simple mouse click. This technique effectively prevents any unauthorized person from reading your protected documents.

The second part of the plan is to *hide* the file itself. Although the contents of a sensitive document may be unreadable, the file can be located and it will be apparent that you are keeping this matter secret. Rather than arousing curiosity, it is better to hide the file so that it cannot be discovered by normal search techniques. Software which hides a document effectively breaks down the contents and scatters the material in different locations within the computer's memory. When you enter your password, the data is reassembled. Matters that you need to maintain on your computer, such as accounting records and other vital information, should be encrypted and hid from view.

The third element of the plan is to destroy information that you don't need to keep. Destroying a document means that it is erased and removed from each area of the computer where it has been stored. Once data is destroyed, it cannot be recovered even by investigative search techniques.

Is a Limited Liability Company different from a Family Limited Partnership?

An LLC is a superior method for holding any Dangerous Asset—capable of producing liability. The problem with the FLP is that the general partners are responsible for the debts of the company. If liability is produced from an asset—for example a rental property—the general partner must personally satisfy the amount of the obligation out of his own assets. In contrast, if the property is held by an LLC, then no member is liable for any debt. The law provides that a member cannot be sued in connection with a liability of the LLC. The risk associated with the property is properly contained and insulated in the LLC.

The same distinction applies concerning the operation of a business. The FLP should never operate a business because of the potential liability of the general partner. The business should always be conducted in the LLC format to protect the owners from the risks associated with the business.

Additionally, several states permit the formation of single member LLCs. One person can own all of the interests. A limited partnership must always have at least two members, which may be inconvenient in some situations.

Is an LLC better than an FLP for protecting financial privacy?

The FLP creates problems if your objective is financial privacy. The name of the general partner must be disclosed on the certificate which is filed with the state. That provides accessible and valuable information to anyone searching for your assets. If you are using an FLP for estate planning or other purposes, it may be best to substitute an LLC as the general partner. That strategy would effectively conceal your name and relationship to the FLP.

Does the FLP have any advantages over the LLC?

The FLP may provide certain estate planning advantages. For those with large estates, exceeding the exemption amount, a gift of limited partnership interests to family members can reduce estate taxes by a substantial degree. Although the same result can probably be obtained with a properly drafted LLC, the issue has not been settled.

What are the objectives of an asset protection plan?

1. **Discourage litigation.** An asset protection plan is designed to discourage a potential lawsuit before it begins. In the ordinary course of litigation, the attorney for the plaintiff will want to make sure that sufficient assets of the defendant can be reached if the litigation is successful. This is especially true when the attorney is working for a contingent fee. Accordingly, prior to commencing a lawsuit, the plaintiff's attorney will perform a financial investigation of your assets, seeking to locate any real estate, bank accounts, or other valuable property. If you have substantial, reachable assets, the lawsuit will go forward. If the investigation reveals that your assets are not in a form that can be seized, only the most self-destructive plaintiff would incur the expense of proceeding with the case.

2. **Allow access to funds prior to trial.** In many types of litigation, the plaintiff can obtain from the court a *Pre-Judgment Writ of Attachment* or a restraining order effectively freezing all

of your funds pending the outcome of the case. This is often the single most potent weapon available to the plaintiff. Without access to funds to meet your business and personal expenses, you will not be able to survive financially during the lawsuit. This tactic will usually force you to enter into an unfavorable settlement regardless of the merits of your defense.

The objective of an asset protection plan is to make sure that your property cannot be tied up in this manner in the event of litigation. An appropriate plan should be designed to keep real estate assets free of attachments and liens and should allow you to maintain undisturbed access to your funds during the litigation process.

3. **Allow access to funds after judgment.** If you are sued and there is a judgment against you, your real estate and bank accounts will be effectively frozen. You will not be able to sell or refinance your property or use your funds to meet your needs and obligations. When assets are legally protected from seizure, your negotiating leverage and ability to dictate the terms of any potential settlement will be dramatically enhanced.

If I use an asset protection plan, can I cancel my liability insurance?

We do not recommend that clients cancel any existing liability policies which they have. One reason for maintaining the liability coverage is that you want the insurance company to pay for your legal defense in the event that you are sued. If you do not have insurance coverage, you will have to pay for your legal fees out of your own pocket. An alternative to paying your own legal costs would be to do nothing to defend the lawsuit, permitting the plaintiff to take a judgment by default in the case. Although assets may be protected from the judgment creditor, it will be possible for the creditor to garnish wages, attach future income, or restrict access to funds through the charging order procedure. If you have an arguable legal defense to the plaintiff's suit, it is better to have your day in court and attempt to win the lawsuit in order to avoid the consequences of having a judgment against you.

What is a fraudulent conveyance?

A fraudulent conveyance is a transfer which is intended to hinder, delay, or defraud a creditor from the collection of his debt. A transfer which is made with an actual intent to defraud a creditor or which renders the transferor insolvent will be considered to be a fraudulent conveyance. A transfer which is a fraudulent conveyance can be set aside by the creditor. In determining whether you have made a fraudulent conveyance, the court will focus on both an objective and a subjective test. The objective test is based upon whether the transfer rendered you insolvent. Generally, insolvency means an inability to meet current debts as they become due. Also, the court will use a balance sheet test to determine if after the transfer, your liabilities exceeded your assets.

The subjective test is based upon your intent at the time of the transfer. Under this test, the business purposes for establishing the asset protection plan will be scrutinized. For example, if a significant motivation for establishing the plan was to accomplish various estate planning objectives, such as providing a mechanism for giving gifts to one's children, a creditor would have a difficult time establishing a fraudulent intent.

Ultimately the issue will really come down to one of timing. Was the transfer made in such close proximity to a lawsuit or a judgment that an intent to defraud is the only credible finding? Clearly, the greater the distance between a transfer and a lawsuit, the stronger the argument that the predominant motivation was not fraudulent as to a particular creditor. Regardless of the timing, asset protection cannot be used as a device to defraud creditors or to avoid paying legitimate obligations.

How do the new filing requirements for foreign trusts affect the Asset Protection Trust?

An Asset Protection Trust can be designed so that it is not treated as a foreign trust for income tax purposes. The trust document must be carefully drawn in order to produce this result. At the point in the future when, because of a potential litigation threat, significant assets are transferred from the U.S. to the overseas trust account, at that time the filings may be necessary. Again, the filing requirement depends upon the way that the trust agreement is structured. Your tax advisor should review the trust agreement to ensure proper compliance with applicable rules.

Can you provide a summary of how all of the pieces of the Privacy Trust plan fit together?

Here is an example of how the Privacy Trust plan operates from a practical standpoint. James and Mary Prudence have accumulated a nest egg of $200,000 for their retirement. Together they own and operate a fast food restaurant. They want maximum privacy for their savings and the business as well as protection from any type of lawsuit or claim. It was decided that they would use a Privacy Trust–Plan #2.

The first step is to transfer the restaurant into an LLC. This is the best arrangement for holding Dangerous Assets, such as an operating business. The LLC protects James and Mary from any liability associated with the restaurant. Similarly, this asset is protected from any outside claim, which may be brought against them.

A second LLC is created to hold their savings in a brokerage account. This provides excellent legal protection of the funds from any claim against James or Mary.

The membership interests in both of the LLCs are held by the Privacy Trust. Accounts are opened in the name of the trust, and the trust company acts as signatory. The trust company executes documents as instructed by James and Mary.

This arrangement does not have any income tax or gift tax consequences. All dividend or interest income earned by the trust or the LLCs is reported on James' and Mary's income tax return. There are no tax savings or disadvantages.

Similarly, there are no gift tax consequences. Since James and Mary have full control over their property, there are no gift tax implications to this setup.

Now let's see what happens if there is ever someone who is thinking about suing James or Mary. As we have seen, the plaintiff's lawyer will want to know whether it is worth his time and money to pursue James and Mary in a lawsuit. When the lawyer performs an asset search, he is unable to locate any property in their names, since they have previously transferred their property to the LLCs held by the Privacy Trust. It is unlikely that he would proceed at this point.

But let's say that the lawsuit is filed and James and Mary lose. Now what happens? Remember, after the lawsuit, the collection process begins with a debtor's examination, with detailed questions concerning the sources of income and the location of assets. Clearly, if James and Mary had *not* transferred their assets into the plan, the judgment creditor would simply have levied on their bank accounts and taken all of their retirement savings. There would be no room to negotiate and no leverage to attempt to work out a deal or a payment schedule. Under normal circumstances, a creditor with a judgment holds all of the cards.

Now the situation is quite different. James and Mary will truthfully answer all of the questions in the judgment debtor's exam. They will state that they are the beneficiaries of the trust. Again, the purpose of the arrangement is not dependent on hiding or concealing assets from a creditor. The plan allows you to answer all questions truthfully and completely.

Now that the plaintiff knows how the assets are held, what does he do? Will he be able to collect on his judgment? The plaintiff would like to seize the cash and the restaurant, but he cannot do that. As we have discussed, a creditor is not permitted to reach assets held in this manner.

At this point, the creditor will certainly be willing to settle for pennies on the dollar. James and Mary can now choose to settle on their terms, if they wish. Or they can choose not to pay any settlement at all. As a practical matter, James and Mary have produced a successful result. They have adopted a plan which discouraged most lawsuits, shielded their valuable assets, and guaranteed that their retirement nest egg is secure.

Index

About the Authors

ROBERT J. MINTZ is an attorney and financial writer specializing in asset protection and privacy matters. He is a member of the California Bar and has practiced law in southern California since 1979. Mintz is a graduate of the University of California, Berkeley (A.B. 1974), The University of San Diego School of Law (J.D. 1978), and Boston University School of Law (LL.M Taxation 1979).

Mintz has written extensively and taught in the areas of financial privacy, asset protection, and estate planning. He is the co-author of the popular and influential book *Lawsuit Proof: Protecting Your Assets from Lawsuits and Claims*. He lives with his family and works in Del Mar, California.

PETER S. DOFT has been practicing law in San Diego County since 1979. Doft received his Bachelor of Arts degree from New York University and his law degree, Summa Cum Laude, from the New England School of Law. He is a member of the Bar in California, New York, and Massachusetts, and has appeared before the United States Supreme Court. He has been a trial attorney for many years and now devotes his law practice exclusively to estate planning and asset protection matters.